Plays on a
COMIC
THEME

Plays on a

COMIC THEME

BUTTERFLIES ARE FREE
A THOUSAND CLOWNS
RINSE THE BLOOD OFF MY TOGA

Edited by
Cy Groves

McGRAW-HILL RYERSON
Toronto   Montreal   New York   St. Louis   San Francisco
Auckland   Beirut   Bogotá   Düsseldorf   Johannesburg
Lisbon   London   Lucerne   Madrid   Mexico   New Delhi
Panama   Paris   San Juan   São Paulo   Singapore   Sydney
Tokyo

PLAYS ON A COMIC THEME

ISBN 0-07-082923-3
     3 4 5 6 7 8 9 0 D 8 7 6 5 4 3 2

Printed and Bound in Canada

Cover Design and Illustrations: Brian F. Reynolds

Cover Photograph: Bob Wood

Canadian Cataloguing in Publication Data

Main entry under title:

Plays on a comic theme

Contents: Gershe, L. Butterflies are free.—Gardner, H. A thousand
clowns.—Wayne, J. and Shuster, F. Rinse the blood off my toga.

ISBN 0-07-082923-3

1. American drama—20th century. 2. Canadian drama—20th century.
3. American drama (Comedy) 4. Canadian drama (Comedy) I. Groves, Cy.
II. Gershe, Leonard. Butterflies are free. III. Gardner, Herb, 1934-   A
thousand clowns. IV. Wayne, Johnny. Rinse the blood off my toga.

PS634.P53   812'.052   C78-001564-9

Acknowledgements:
A Thousand Clowns, by Herb Gardner, Copyright © 1961, 1962, by Herb Gardner and
Irwin A. Cantor, Trustee. Reprinted by permission of Random House, Inc.

Butterflies Are Free, by Leonard Gershe, Copyright © 1969, 1970, by Leonard Gershe. Reprinted by permission of Random House, Inc. Adapted for use in this anthology.

Rinse the Blood Off My Toga, by Johnny Wayne and Frank Shuster, Copyright © 1955, by
Johnny Wayne and Frank Shuster. Reprinted by permission of North Productions.

The photographs for *Butterflies Are Free* and *A Thousand Clowns* are from Museum of
Modern Art/Film Stills Archive.

The photographs for *Rinse the Blood Off My Toga* are from Harold Whyte Photography,
Toronto.

CONTENTS

INTRODUCTION

Almost everyone welcomes the joy and laughter of comedy. Young and old alike flock to motion pictures that advertise an evening of laughter and humour. At home we switch television channels to situation comedies as a welcome change from the world's problems. Sold-out notices are posted outside theatres that present plays or musicals labelled "comedy."

This book of comedy scripts is designed especially for high school students who want to enjoy and understand comedy. In the pages that follow you will find opportunities to:

—practise comedy playwriting,
—produce humorous sketches, parodies, and short plays for classroom presentation,
—present Readers' Theatre versions of plays and poems,
—understand the thoughts and techniques of comedy.

Two full-length comedies have been chosen because both have been successful stage plays and motion pictures that helped us to laugh at the ways younger and older people think, feel, and live: *Butterflies Are Free* and *A Thousand Clowns*.

Also included is the Shakespearian parody, *Rinse the Blood Off My Toga*, by the Canadian humorists, Johnny Wayne and Frank Shuster. This play has been included as an example of one kind of comedy, parody, that makes fun of a particular piece of literature through imitation of the familiar story line. Parody uses a technique of humour similar to the take-offs in *Mad Magazine*, and to the spoofs on television variety programs. Because this technique lends itself to original writing, it provides the chance to write and produce classroom or school comedy at the amateur level.

A variety of approaches to responding to plays are included, ranging from traditional dramatic analysis to writing and acting humorous sketches.

You are meant to laugh your way through these comedies. At the same time, you will be given a chance to practise writing skills related to comedy sketches and organizational skills related to Readers' Theatre presentations. From your involvement with these plays, you will come to understand and enjoy plays with a comic theme.

1

What Makes A
COMEDY COMICAL?

Comedy is as old as laughter and as modern as the most current life style. Comedy deals with the most interesting of topics—life itself. No person, place, or subject is sacred where comedy is concerned. Marriage, the generation gap, war, detective stories, prejudice, young love, old love, schools, and teachers have all been used as the subjects for comedy. Comedy has one major purpose: to hold up a critical mirror to life through humour, with a happy ending.

Using man's imperfections as its target, comedy has taken for its themes such human conflicts as:
—the war of the life styles,
—the battle of the sexes,
—the differences between generations,
—racial differences,
—the differences between single and married life,
—the conflicting opinions in the medical world.

In class discussion, suggest some of the television comedies that have used any of these conflicts for creating humour. Add suggestions of your own to the list of conflicts above. Now match your suggestions to plays, musicals, motion pictures, or television comedies with which you are familiar.

3

Although the popularity of certain topics at which comedy pokes fun may change a little with each generation, the techniques of comedy seem to remain constant. These techniques involve the use of the following seven basic devices:

The incongruous
A teacher riding into class on a donkey

The "caught in the act" slice of life
A young man nonchalantly places a slug into the bus coin box, but puts his hand in too far and cannot get it out.

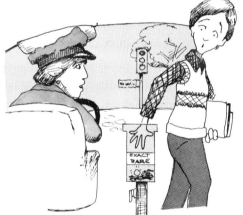

The ridiculous
A psychiatrist looking at a chimpanzee through an observation hole in the lab wall and seeing an eye

E
x
a
g
g
e
r
a
t
i
o
n

The exaggerated facial and body gestures of the silent movies produce laughter in today's audience.

Bathos: The sudden unexpected switch from the serious to the comical

A happy fly buzzes the 11 o'clock news announcer as the show goes on the air.

Wit: the quick expression of a surprising, humorous remark

If life hands you a lemon . . . make lemonade!

Stereotyped comic characters who look and/or sound comical

The offbeat "kooky" personality

The loser

A writer of comedy also employs the following literary styles to produce humour:

Parody or humorous imitation of a piece of literature

Rinse the Blood Off My Toga humorously imitates the Shakespearian play *Julius Caesar*.

Satire or the ridiculing of individuals, customs, ideas, or states of affairs for the purpose of achieving humor and/or reform

A Thousand Clowns ridicules the world of conformity and the 9-5 rat race of many working people.

Farce or the use of far-fetched situations and behaviour usually involving stereotyped characters

Rinse the Blood Off My Toga uses a chariot race when Flavius chases Brutus.

Build up a class inventory of comedy devices and literary styles. Use segments of familiar motion pictures, television programs, plays, as well as real-life situations, to find your examples of characters and situations that are humorous. By doing this you will develop a first-hand understanding of the kinds of things that make comedy comical.

Introduction to
BUTTERFLIES ARE FREE

Critics were filled with praise for both the play and the motion picture version of *Butterflies Are Free*:

"Should have audiences laughing for months to come."

"A load of laughs."

"Heartwarming comedy."

The subject seemed an unusual one for comedy: blindness. The young sympathized readily with the young, blind boy escaping to his own "pad" from an overprotective mother. The older generation related to the stern but very concerned mother with the heart of gold beneath the tough exterior.

The author, Leonard Gershe, used as inspiration a radio interview with a blind law student whose draft board had classified him medically unable to serve. The author recalled how he "had never met a blind person, and was bowled over by this boy's humour and healthy attitude about his situation." Mr. Gershe had a friend who was afraid of committing herself to any permanent, friendly relationship with another person, and used this character as well in his play. He brought these two experiences of real people together as the base for his comedy.

Before reading, acting, or videotaping a student production, it is a good idea to "warm up" your mind in order to enjoy and appreciate this play. The following questions are designed to encourage discussion as a warm-up prior to experiencing *Butterflies Are Free*:

1. Actors try to "crawl into the skin" of the character they are portraying in order to become that person. How do you think one can learn to "crawl into the skin" of another person?

2. Most characters in plays, as well as people in real life, have been said to be like icebergs, one-tenth of them shows on the surface while nine-tenths are hidden. Share your individual experiences of this theory by recalling people you have known or by using characters from books, plays, motion pictures, or television programs.

3. A character in a play, and people in real life, reveal themselves by:
   —what they say,
   —what they do,
   —what they think,
   —what others say about them,
   —how they react to others.

Using only positive comments, show how individuals in the class (volunteers) send out character "vibrations" as a result of the above five methods of revealing characterization.

4. A playwright often applies the old saying "Appearances are deceptive" in order to surprise an audience. Be prepared for this to happen in *Butterflies Are Free*, where you will probably change your minds about the main characters as you read the play. Share class experiences of how first impressions of someone you were introduced to were changed when you got to know that person better.

5. You can tell a great deal about a person by looking at that person's surroundings. This happens in a play when the curtain first opens and you come to conclusions about the characters from the details of the setting. Those of you who have visited your friends' homes could share with the class how a person's room can tell a great deal about that individual. Bring to class a snapshot of your own study room for a class collage of students' home settings. Try to match the setting with its student occupant from your class.

CASTING THE PLAY FOR A PLAY-READING OR WALKTHROUGH PRODUCTION

Play-reading: reading the dialogue as dramatically as possible using individual students "cast" by the class, with your teacher reading the non-dialogue sections.

Walkthrough production: similar to play-reading but with the addition of hand-held play scripts, and the use of the front of the class as an acting area. Movement, gesture, facial expression, and simple props accompany the dramatic reading of the dialogue.

Before the play-reading or the walkthrough production of *Butterflies Are Free*, it is a good idea for the whole class to suggest who would probably be able to project well each character in the play. The following brief notes on the play's characters will help you to cast the play. They are the kind of quick descriptions a casting director might have in mind when choosing actors for their roles.

DON BAKER
—twenty years old
—cheerful
—intelligent
—sympathetic
—honest
—has a good sense of humour

—patient
—affectionate
—independent

JILL TANNER
—nineteen years old
—kittenish
—"kooky"
—scatterbrained
—a "flower child" kind of person
—a person who meant to go to university but "couldn't find a parking
  space"
—afraid of getting emotionally involved with people

MRS. BAKER
—Don's overprotective mother
—witty
—a woman who doesn't want to see her son get hurt in life
—she has a heart of gold underneath the exterior "squareness"
—she likes things neat, tidy, and orderly
—she speaks her mind

RALPH AUSTIN (small part in Act Two only)
—a sloppily dressed play director
—noisy
—a way-out rebel who likes to direct plays that shock people
—a man who is critical of the conservative, older generation
—an odd type

The cast could be changed for each act. Besides play-reading and
walkthroughs of the play, additional methods of experiencing the play
could be used.

READERS' THEATRE

One of the most popular ways of presenting dramatic material in the
classroom is through the use of Readers' Theatre. Students simply sit on
high stools facing the rest of the class and read from the play script using
voice, facial expression, and gesture to bring the written words off the
page. In this way the stress of memorizing lines and movements is
avoided but much of the play's intensity is maintained through well-
prepared vocal interpretation of the lines.

The following elements involved in "covering the script" dramatically have proved to be the most successful for Readers' Theatre presentation:

1. The whole play script is divided into 15-20 minute segments in order,
   from beginning to end. Individual groups from the class are assigned

these segments of the play in order. Under their chosen director, members of the group prepare their Readers' Theatre production for presentation in front of the class.

2. Each character in his or her segment of the play is first discussed by the group who try to extract the character's thoughts, beliefs, and feelings from the 15-20 minute segment of the script. A narrator provides transition between scenes by announcing time and scene changes.

3. Alternatively to the whole play script method, only highlight scenes from the play are extracted and assigned to groups from the class for Readers' Theatre presentation.

4. In the case of a short play, a single group presents its Readers' Theatre presentation. The rest of the class play-reads and discusses the play while the single group is in rehearsal.

5. A "stream of consciousness" presentation: In most situations we speak only a tiny part of what is going on in our minds. A person being criticized by his or her boss will probably not say what is on his or her mind. In a "stream of consciousness" presentation, each character in the script is played by two people. One speaks the actual words in the script; the other says what the character is *really* thinking. The inner thoughts of the character are worked out by the group ahead of time. This is to make sure that two people are not speaking at the same time.

The following staging suggestions are provided as hints for improving Readers' Theatre presentations:

1. Every play has two sides. Decide which characters are on which side and seat the two sides so that they face each other.

2. Plays are not democratic; some characters are more important than others. Show this in your seating arrangement by having the more important characters seated on a higher level than the others.

3. In a staged play, a character can walk off stage. In Readers' Theatre s/he can't do this, but s/he can sit with his or her back turned to show that s/he is not part of that particular scene.

4. You may wish to use a narrator if you are leaving out some of the scenes and you want to tell the audience about what was left out. If you want someone to read out stage directions, you may wish to use a narrator as well. Seating the narrator to one side of the group will help to show that s/he is not a character in the play.

5. Different kinds of plot can be represented in your seating arrangements. For example, when two men are in love with one woman or two women are in love with one man, we call this an eternal triangle. If such a triangle were the subject of your play, you could seat your characters so that the involved persons were at the three points of a triangle.

Many other variations are possible and are best discovered by trying out different groupings during rehearsals.

Although the human voice is the primary skill in Readers' Theatre, additional dramatic devices may be used to increase the effectiveness of the spoken word.

How to obtain variety of spoken delivery

Change the speed and rhythm for emphasis, mood, and understanding.

Use dramatic pauses for emphasis, suspense, and intensity.

Change the volume from a stage whisper to a loud cry for interpretation.

Change the vocal tone from soft and gentle to hard and blunt for suggesting character traits and for helping the audience to understand the meaning.

Use accent or dialect to suggest, for example, a specific nationality or social class.

How to use setting

Use a simple, uncluttered rear wall as a neutral backdrop.

Position a cut-out tree, high-rise building, or bookcase, to suggest a significant element in the setting for the play.

How to use lighting

Project different coloured lighting to produce a mood that fits the subject of the play.

Use spotlighted acting area "pools" to suggest specific locations into which characters can move with their stools.

How to use costume

Dress all members of the group in similar neutral costumes such as dark slacks and white sweaters for final presentation in front of the class.

Add the following simple elements to suggest the character being portrayed: hat, scarf, wig, coat, gloves, tie, necklace, and earrings.

How to use music

Set the mood with music for the introduction and for the conclusion. Indicate transition between scenes with appropriate theme music.

How to use sound effects

Use only if essential to the dialogue (e.g., doorbell, bird song, clock striking).

During the rehearsals the emphasis should be on:

—speaking the lines in such a way as to get the meaning across;

—stressing those words and phrases that are key idea elements;

—using voices that best match the kind of character being portrayed;

—looking up from the script as much as possible in order to avoid being buried in the pages;

—matching speed, volume, tone, pitch, and rhythm to the character and to the meaning of the words;

—bringing the play to life by living the roles being portrayed.

GROUP PRESENTATIONS

Using the Readers' Theatre type of presentation, break down the play into self-contained sections and have each group present its own prepared version.

MINI-PRODUCTIONS

Use the group presentation format but choose only highlight scenes of two to three pages of script. Present an acted version of the play (no scripts in hand) following group rehearsals. A director should be chosen from within the group. Include whatever elements of setting, lighting, costumes, make-up, music, and sound effects are available or possible.

BUTTERFLIES ARE FREE

Leonard Gershe

THE SCENE

The entire action takes place in DON BAKER'S
apartment on East 11th Street in New York City.

Act One

Scene 1: A morning in June.
Scene 2: A few hours later.

Act Two

Scene 1: A moment later.
Scene 2: That night.

Act One

SCENE ONE

The scene is DON BAKER'S *apartment on the top floor of a walk-up on the Lower East Side of Manhattan. There is a skylight, dirty with age. The bed is raised about six and a half feet from the floor, and is reached by a ladder. Under the bed is a door leading to the bathroom. We can make out some posters and photographs pinned to the wall. To the left of the bed is the front door; to the right is the kitchen, with a vintage refrigerator and an old claw-foot bathtub. A slab of wood has been fitted over the tub to serve as a dining table; a couple of stools are around it. Just below the table-tub there is a faded sofa. In front of this is a wood crate which serves as a coffee table, with some cheap chairs around it. There is a telephone on the coffee table. On one wall is a window and a small bookcase. There is a second door, which leads to the next apartment; in front of it is a chest.*

Before the curtain rises we hear DON BAKER'S *voice singing on a tape recorder: "I knew the day you met me/I could love you if you let me/Though you touched my cheek/And said how easy you'd forget me/You said (Improvising) da-de-da-de-da-da . . ."**

When the curtain rises it is a warm morning in June; the sun is pouring in through the skylight. DON *is leaning against one of the bedposts, drinking a glass of water, and listening to the tape recorder. He is twenty years old, lean and good-looking, wearing a brown button-down shirt and khakis; his hair is combed back and his feet are bare. The phone rings. He moves to the sofa, turns off the tape recorder, looks toward the phone, and speaks to it in a tone indicating he has said this many times.*

DON: I'm fine, thank you. How are you? *(He goes to the kitchen, and refills his glass with water)* It's warm here. How is it in Scarsdale? *(Goes to the phone)* Well, it's warm here, too. *(Picks up the phone)* Hello, Mother . . . I just knew. When you call, the phone doesn't ring. It just says, "M" is for the million things she gave you . . . I'm fine, thank you. How are you? . . . It's warm here. How is it in Scarsdale? . . . Well, it's warm here, too. The apartment is great. I love it . . . Last night? I didn't do anything last night. I mean I didn't go out. I had some friends in—a little party . . . I don't know how many people were here. Do you have to have a number? Twelve and a half, how's that? . . . No, they didn't stay too late . . . When? No! No, not this afternoon . . . I don't care. Come to town and go to Saks, but you're not coming down here. Because we agreed to two months, didn't we? *(Suddenly the noise of a conversational TV program is heard blaring in the next apartment)* What? . . . No, I didn't turn on my radio. It's coming from next door . . . I don't know . . . a girl . . . She just moved in a couple of days ago . . . I don't know her name. I haven't met her . . . It's her radio . . . Don't worry, it won't go on . . . Yes, I'll tell her . . . No, I don't want you to tell her. Just go to Saks and go home . . . I can hardly hear you. We'll talk tomorrow. Good-bye. *(DON hangs up, goes to the door that connects with the next apartment, and raps angrily)* Hey, would you please . . . *(Knocking louder and shouting)* Would you mind lowering your radio?

(The TV program is turned off)

JILL *(Offstage)*: Sorry, I couldn't hear you.

DON: I just wanted you to turn your radio down. You don't have to turn it off. Just lower it, please.

JILL *(Offstage)*: I haven't got a radio. It's television.

DON: Well, whatever. These walls are made of paper.

JILL *(Offstage)*: I know—Kleenex. How about a cup of coffee?

DON: No, thanks. I just had some.

JILL *(Offstage)*: I meant for me.

DON: Sure . . . come on in. *(DON goes to the kitchen and turns on the flame under the coffee pot. There is a knock at the door as he takes a cup and saucer from the cupboard over the sink)* It's open.

(JILL TANNER enters. She is nineteen and has a delicate little-girl quality about her. Her long hair falls to her shoulders and down her back. She is wearing an arty blouse and blue jeans. Her blouse zips down the back, and the top of the zipper is open)

JILL: Hi! I'm Jill Tanner.

DON: *(Turning toward her and extending his hand)* Don Baker.

(JILL shakes his hand)

JILL: I hope you don't mind me inviting myself in. *(Turning her back to him)* Would you do the zipper on my blouse? I can't reach back there. *(There is just a flash of awkwardness as DON reaches out for the zipper and zips it up)* Your living room is bigger than mine. How long have you been here?

DON: A month. This isn't the living room. This is the apartment. That's all there is except I have a big bathroom.

JILL: I've got three rooms if you count the kitchen. I just moved in two days ago, but I didn't sign a lease or anything—just by the month. God, you're neat. Everything is so tidy.

DON: It's easy when you haven't got anything.

JILL *(Looking around)*: I haven't got anything, but it manages to wind up all over the place. I'm afraid I'm a slob. I've heard that boys are neater than girls. *(Looking up)* I like your skylight. I don't have that. *(Moves to the bed)* What's this?

DON: What?

JILL: This thing on stilts.

DON: Oh, my bed.

JILL *(Climbing the ladder)*: Your bed? Wow! This is WILD!

DON: Do you like it?

JILL *(Climbing on the bed)*: This is the greatest bed I've ever seen in my life . . . and I've seen a lot of beds. Did you build it?

DON: No, the guy who lived here before me built it. He was a hippie. He liked to sleep high.

JILL: Suppose you fall out? You could break something.

DON: You could break something falling out of any bed. *(He pours the coffee into the cup, goes to the coffee table and sets it down)* Cream or sugar?

JILL: No, just black.

DON: I could have had your apartment, but I took this one because of the bed.

JILL: I don't blame you. *(Moving to the sofa)* You know, I buy flowers and dumb things like dishtowels and paper napkins, but I keep forgetting to buy coffee.
   (JILL settles on the sofa with her feet beneath her. She picks up the coffee and sips it)
DON: Is it hot enough?
JILL: Great. This'll save my life. I'll pay you back some day.
DON: You don't have to.
JILL: Do you need any dishtowels or paper napkins?
DON: No.
JILL: I've got lots of light bulbs, too—everything but coffee. May I ask you a personal question?
DON: Sure.
JILL: Why don't you want your mother to come here?
DON: How did you know that?
JILL: If you can hear me, I can hear you. I think the sound must go right under that door. What's that door for, anyway?
DON: Your apartment and mine were once one apartment. When they converted it into two, they just locked that door instead of sealing it up. I guess in case they want to make it one again.
JILL: You didn't answer my question.
DON: I forgot what you asked.
JILL: Why don't you want your mother here?
DON: It's a long story. No, it's a short story—it's just been going on a long time. She didn't want me to leave home. She thinks I can't make it on my own. Finally, we agreed to letting me try it for two months. She's to keep away from me for two months. I've got a month to go.
JILL: Why did you tell her you had a party last night?
DON: Boy, you don't miss anything in there, do you?
JILL: Not much.
DON: I always tell her I've had a party . . . or went to one. She wouldn't understand why I'd rather be here alone than keeping her and the cook company. She'll hate this place. She hates it now without even seeing it. She'll walk in and the first thing she'll say is, "I could absolutely cry!"
JILL: Does she cry a lot?
DON: No—she just threatens to.
JILL: If she really wants to cry, send her in to look at my place. At least you're neat. You're old enough to live alone, aren't you? I'm nineteen. How old are you?
DON: As far as my mother's concerned, I'm still eleven—going on ten.
JILL: We must have the same mother. Mine would love me to stay a child all my life—or at least all *her* life. So *she* won't age. She loves it when people say we look like sisters. If they don't say it, she tells them. Have you got a job?
DON: Not yet . . . but I play the guitar, and I've got a few prospects.
JILL: I heard you last night.
DON: Sorry.
JILL: No, it was good. First I thought it was a record till you kept playing one song over and over.
DON: I can't read music, so I have to learn by ear. I'm trying to put together an act.
JILL: Then what?
DON: Then I'll try to cash in on some of those prospects. I know one thing—I ain't a-goin' back to Scarsdale.
JILL: What is Scarsdale?

DON: You don't know Scarsdale?

JILL: I don't know much about the East. I'm from Los Angeles.

DON: Scarsdale's just outside of New York—about twenty miles.

JILL: Is that where you live?

DON: No, I live here. It's where I used to live.

JILL: Scars-dale. It sounds like a sanitarium where they do plastic surgery. Is there any more coffee?

DON *(Putting his cigarette out in the ashtray)*: Plenty.

JILL: I can get it.

DON *(Rises and holds out his hand for the cup)*: I'm up. (JILL *hands him the cup. He goes to the kitchen to pour her more coffee)* What did you say your name is?

JILL: Jill Tanner. Technically, I guess I'm Mrs. Benson. I was married once . . . when I was sixteen.

DON: Sixteen! Did you have your parents' permission?

JILL: My mother's. I told her I was pregnant, but I wasn't. She cried her eyes out. She hated the thought of becoming a grandmother. I'll bet I know what you're thinking.

DON: What?

(DON *returns, sets the cup on the table, and resumes his seat)*

JILL: You're thinking I don't look like a *divorcée*.

DON: No, I wasn't thinking that. What does a divorcée look like?

JILL: Oh, you know. They're usually around thirty-five with tight-fitting dresses and high-heel patent leather shoes and big boobs. I look more like the kid in a custody fight.

DON: How long were you married?

JILL: God, it seemed like weeks! Actually, it was six days. *(She lights a cigarette)* It wasn't Jack's fault. It wasn't anybody's fault. It was just one of those terrible mistakes you make before you can stop yourself, even though you know it's a mistake while you're doing it.

DON: What was he like?

JILL: Jack? Oh . . . *(Uncomfortably)* I really can't talk about him.

DON: Then don't. I'm sorry.

JILL: No, I will talk about him. Once in a while it's good for you to do something you don't want to do. It cleanses the insides. He was terribly sweet and groovy-looking, but kind of adolescent, you know what I mean? Girls mature faster than boys. Boys are neater, but girls mature faster. When we met it was like fireworks and rockets. I don't know if I'm saying it right, but it was a marvelous kind of passion that made every day like the Fourth of July. Anyway, the next thing I knew we were standing in front of a justice of the peace getting married.

DON: How long had you known him?

JILL: Two or three weeks, but I mean there we were getting *married*! I hadn't even finished high school and I had two exams the next day and they were on my mind, too. I heard the justice of the peace saying, "Do you, *Jack*, take Jill to be your lawfully wedded wife?" Can you imagine going through life as Jack and Jill? And then I heard "Till death do you part," and suddenly it wasn't a wedding ceremony. It was a funeral service.

DON *(Lighting a cigarette)*: Jesus!

JILL: You know, that wedding ceremony is very morbid when you think about it. I

hate anything morbid and there I was being buried alive . . . under Jack Benson.
I wanted to run screaming out into the night!

DON: Did you?

JILL: I couldn't. It was ten o'clock in the morning. I mean you can't go screaming out
into ten o'clock in the morning—so I passed out. If only I'd fainted before I said
"I do."

DON: As long as you were married, why didn't you try to make it work?

JILL: I did try—believe me. *(She picks up an ashtray and holds it in her hand)* I tried
for six days, but I knew it was no good.

DON: Were you in love with him?

> *(DON flicks an ash from his cigarette onto the table where the ashtray had
> been before JILL moved it. JILL reacts to this fleetingly, and shrugs it off)*

JILL: In my way.

DON: What's your way?

JILL: I don't know . . . Well, I think just because you love someone, that doesn't necessarily mean that you want to spend the rest of your life with him. But Jack
loved me. I mean he really, really loved me, and I hurt him and that's what I can't
stand. I just never want to hurt anybody. I mean marriage is a commitment, isn't
it? I just can't be committed or involved. Can you understand?

DON: I understand, but I don't agree.

> *(DON flicks his ashes onto the table)*

JILL: Then you don't understand really. *(JILL looks at him, oddly)* What is this?
Maybe I've got it wrong. Maybe boys mature faster and girls are neater.

DON: What do you mean?

JILL: Or maybe you know something I don't know—like ashes are good for the
table? Is that why you keep dropping them there?

DON: Did you move the ashtray?

JILL *(Holding up the ashtray beside her)*: It's right here. Are you blind?

DON: Yes.

JILL: What do you mean *yes?*

DON: I mean yes. I'm blind.

JILL: You're putting me on.

DON: No, I'm blind. I've always been blind.

JILL: Really blind? Not just near-sighted?

DON: The works. I can't see a thing.

> *(JILL leans over and runs her hands across DON's eyes. When he doesn't
> blink, she realizes he is indeed blind)*

JILL: God! I hope I didn't say anything . . .

DON: Now, don't get self-conscious about it. I'm not.

JILL: Why didn't you tell me?

DON: I just did.

JILL: I mean when I came in.

DON: You didn't ask me.

JILL: Why would I ask? I mean I don't go into someone's house and say, "Hi, I'm Jill
Tanner—are you blind?"

DON: Right. And I don't meet a stranger and say, "Hi, Don Baker—blind as a bat."

JILL: I think you should've told me. I would've told you.

DON: Well . . . I wanted to see how long it would take for you to catch on. Now you
know. Do you want to run screaming out into the night or just faint?

JILL: How can you make jokes?

DON: Listen, the one thing that drives me up the wall is pity. I don't want it and I don't need it. Please—don't feel sorry for me. I don't feel sorry for me, so why should you?

JILL: You're so . . . adjusted.

DON: No, I'm not. I never *had* to adjust. I was born blind. It might be different if I'd been able to see and then went blind. For me, blindness is normal. I was six years old before I found out everyone else wasn't blind. By that time it didn't make much difference. So, let's relax about it. Okay? And if we can have a few laughs, so much the better.

JILL: A few laughs? About *blindness?*

DON: No, not about blindness. Can't you just forget that?

JILL: I don't know. You're the first blind person I've ever met.

DON: Congratulations. Too bad they don't give out prizes for that.

JILL: I've seen blind men on the street—you know, with dogs. Why don't you have a dog?

DON: They attract too much attention. I'd rather do it myself.

JILL: But isn't it rough getting around New York? It is for me!

DON: Not at all. I manage very well with my cane. I've got so I know exactly how many steps to take to the grocery . . . the laundry . . . the drugstore.

JILL: Where's a laundry? I need one.

DON: Next to the delicatessen. Forty-four steps from the front door.

JILL: I didn't see it.

DON: I'll show it to you.

JILL: What about here in the apartment? Aren't you afraid of bumping into everything? You could hurt yourself.

DON: I've memorized the room. *(Moves around the room with grace and confidence, calling off each item as he touches it or points to it)* Bed . . . bathroom . . . bookcase . . . guitar . . . my cane.
　　　(He holds up the white aluminum walking stick, then puts it back on the shelf)

JILL: What are those books?

DON: Braille . . . Front door . . . tape recorder. *(Moving on)* Dining table . . . bathtub. *(Walks quickly to the chest of drawers against the door to* JILL's *apartment)* Chest of drawers. *(Touching the things on top)* Wine . . . glasses. *(He opens the top drawer)* Linens. *(Closes the drawer; opens the front door and shuts it; moves on to the kitchen)* Kitchen . . . *(He opens the cabinet over the sink)* Dishes . . . cups . . . glasses. *(He opens the next cabinet)* Coffee . . . sugar . . . salt and pepper . . . corn flakes . . . ketchup . . . etcetera. *(Returning to* JILL*)* Now, if you'll put the ashtray back. *(She replaces the ashtray on the table, and* DON *stamps out his cigarette in it. He sits on the sofa and holds out his arms with bravura)* Voilà! If you don't move anything, I'm as good as anyone else.

JILL: Better. God, I can't find anything in my place. The ketchup usually winds up in my stocking drawer and my stockings are in the oven. If you really want to see chaos, come and look at . . . *(She catches herself, self-consciously)* I mean . . . I meant . . .

DON: I know what you mean. Relax. I'm no different from anyone else except that I don't see. The blindness is nothing. The thing I find hard to live with is other people's reactions to my blindness. If they'd only behave naturally. Some people want to assume guilt—which they can't because my mother has that market cornered—or they treat me as though I were living in some Greek tragedy, which I assure you I'm not. Just be yourself.

JILL: I'll try . . . but I've never met a blind person before.

DON: That's because we're a small, very select group—like Eskimos. How many Eskimos do you know?

JILL: I never thought blind people would be like you.

DON: They're not all like me. We're all different.

JILL: I mean . . . I always thought blind people were kind of . . . you know . . . spooky.

DON *(In a mock-sinister voice)*: But, of course. We sleep all day hanging upside-down from the shower rod. As soon as it's dark, we wake up and fly into people's windows. That's why they say, "Blind as a bat."

JILL: No, seriously . . . don't blind people have a sixth sense?

DON: No. If I had six senses, I'd still have only five, wouldn't I? My other senses—hearing, touch, smell—maybe they're a little more developed than yours, but that's only because I use them more. I have to.

JILL: Boy, I think it's just so great that you aren't bitter. You don't seem to have any bitterness at all. *(She shifts to sitting on the sofa, burying her feet under a cushion)* I've moved. I'm sitting on the sofa now.

DON: I know.

JILL: How did you know?

DON: I heard you—and your voice is coming from a different spot.

JILL: Wow! How do you do it?

DON: It's easy. Close your eyes and listen. *(He tiptoes to another part of the room)* You know where I am?

JILL: There. Hey, it works. You're really something. I think I'd be terribly bitter if I couldn't see. I'd sure be disagreeable.

DON: No, you wouldn't.

JILL: I couldn't be cheerful like you. I don't have any marvelous qualities like courage and fortitude.

DON: Neither have I. I'm just naturally adorable.

JILL: You're more than that. I can tell you're a much better person than I am.

DON: Are you speaking to me or Gunga Din?

JILL: I would not "go gentle into that good night." I would "rage against the dying of the light."

DON: Dylan Thomas.

JILL: Who?

DON: That's a line from a poem by Dylan Thomas.

JILL *(Delightfully surprised)*: It is? You mean I can quote from Dylan Thomas?

DON: You just did.

JILL: How about that! I've never even read him. I don't know where I learned it. I can quote Mark Twain. Do you want to hear my favourite quotation? It's by Mark Twain.

DON: Go ahead.

JILL *(Reciting)*: "I only ask to be free. The butterflies are free. Mankind will surely not deny to Harold Skimpole what it concedes to the butterflies." *(Resuming her normal tone)* I identify, strongly, with butterflies. Do you like that quotation?

DON: Yes, but it's not by Mark Twain.

JILL: Why not?

DON: Because it was written by Charles Dickens.

JILL: Are you sure?

DON: Yes. Harold Skimpole is a character in *Bleak House* by Dickens.

JILL: I've never read Dickens. Actually, I've never read anything by Mark Twain, either, but I always thought he wrote that. Have you read . . . *(Gasping)* Oh, God!

DON *(He crosses the room to get his guitar)*: Yes, I've read Dickens and most of the things by Mark Twain, and stop falling apart with every word. They're published in braille.

JILL: But it's awful to ask someone blind if he's read something.

DON: As a matter of fact, I read very well—with my fingertips. Just ask me if I've felt any good books lately.

JILL: Do people ever read to you?

DON: Yes—magazines and newspapers.

JILL: Would you like me to read to you sometime?

DON: Sure—but don't feel you have to. Say, do you have any dirty books?

JILL: No.

DON: Too bad—that's the only thing they don't publish in braille.

JILL: Which magazines do you like?

DON: Things like *Time* and *Newsweek.* I like to know what's going on in the world.

JILL: I should read those, too. I never know what's going on in the world. I guess I don't care.

DON: Don't say that. Animals care. Vegetables don't. You have to care about something or you're nothing.

JILL: Food.

DON: You care about food?

JILL: I think about it a lot.

DON: I suppose that's something.

JILL: You have to know a lot about things to care about them, and I don't really know a lot about anything.

DON: You sure don't need any enemies, do you?

JILL: Let's say I know my limitations.

DON: That's half the battle. If you know your limitations, you can do something about them. I think you have a lot more potential than you know.

JILL: Keep telling me that.

DON: Keep telling yourself that. *(He strums his guitar and sings)*
> *I knew the day you met me*
> *I could love you if you let me,*
> *Though you touched my cheek*
> *And said how easy you'd forget me,*
> *You said, "Butterflies are free*
> *And so are we."*

JILL: Oh, wow. That's wonderful. That's the song you were singing last night.

DON: I wrote it. I've been working on it, but I could never get those last lines right. What do you think?

JILL: It's terrific! I know a little about music. I studied in school.

DON: Did you finish school?

JILL: I finished high school—*just.* My mother wanted me to go to college. I was going to U.C.L.A., but I couldn't find a place to park. Have you ever been to L.A.?

DON: No. I hear the climate is great.

JILL: The climate is great, but the weather is lousy. I guess it's a good place to live—with gardens and pools and all that. I like it better here. People say New York is a great place to visit, but they wouldn't want to live here. What could be groovier than living in a place that's great to visit?

DON: What made you come here?

JILL: Nothing *made* me come. I just thought I'd like to try something different. I think I'm going to be an actress. I say I think. I'll know later this afternoon. I'm reading for a part in a new off-Broadway play.

DON: Good part?

JILL: I guess so. It's the lead. It's about a girl who gets all hung up because she's married a homosexual. Originally he was an alcoholic, but homosexuals are very "in" now, so they changed it. Are you homosexual?

DON: No—just blind.

JILL: They are in everything now—books, plays, movies. It's really too bad. I always thought of them as kind of magical and mysterious—the greatest secret society in the world. Now they're telling all the secrets and you find out they're just like everybody else—mixed up and sad. Do you know any homosexuals?

DON: I doubt it. I've been in Scarsdale all my life.

JILL: One of my best friends is gay. Dennis. He's a designer. He made this blouse.
      (She holds her blouse out for DON to see, then winces to herself)

DON: I'm sure it's pretty.

JILL: Actually, he made it for himself, but I talked him out of it. Dennis is campy and fun, but I don't like lesbians. They're so heavy and humourless. If guys are called "gay," the girls should be called "glum."

DON: Tell me about the play. Does the girl convert the husband?

JILL: Almost, but in the end he runs off with her brother.

DON: So her husband becomes her sister-in-law.

JILL: Something like that. Or she becomes her own sister-in-law. I have a good chance of getting the part. The director is a friend of mine, but I have to be approved by the author.

DON: Who's the director?

JILL: You wouldn't know him. His name is Ralph Austin. He's done a few plays here, but never had a hit. He started in L.A. doing off-Broadway shows on Hollywood Boulevard.

DON: That's what I call off-Broadway.

JILL: We kind of made it together for a few months, but then he wanted to get married. I just couldn't face that again.

DON: Were you in love with him?

JILL: I don't think I've ever really been in love with anyone. I don't want to be. It's so . . . confining and somebody always gets hurt. Are you hungry?

DON: Not very. Are you?

JILL: Always. My appetite embarrasses me. I told you I think about food a lot . . . and care deeply. Why don't I go down to the delicatessen and get something? I know exactly where it is—forty-four steps from the front door.

DON: That's the laundry. The delicatessen is fifty-one steps. *(He rises)* I've got things to eat.

JILL: What have you got?

DON: Some bologna and salami and potato salad—and I think there's some coleslaw.

JILL: Boy, you *are* a delicatessen. Can you shop for yourself?

DON: Sure.

JILL: I mean, I know you can tell a dime from a quarter, but how do you know the difference between a dollar bill and five?
      (DON takes his wallet from his hip pocket and takes out a bill)

DON: This is a single. Right?

JILL: How do you know?

DON: Because it's folded once. If it were a five, I'd fold it again . . . like this. *(He folds the bill again)* And a ten I'd fold once more. *(He folds the bill again to demonstrate, then unfolds it and puts it back in his wallet)* Got it?

JILL: What about twenties?

DON: Who's got twenties?

(DON crosses to the kitchen and sets about putting the food on plates)

JILL: Can I do something?

DON: There are some knives and forks in the chest of drawers. You can set the table.

JILL *(Crossing to the chest)*: Let's don't eat at the table. Let's have a picnic.

DON: Where?

JILL: On the floor.

DON: Okay, set the floor.

(JILL takes the silverware and a small cloth from the chest, and sets them out on the floor in front of the coffee table)

JILL: Is blindness hereditary?

DON: I've never heard that.

JILL: Can your father see?

DON: I doubt it. He's been dead for six years. Up till then he didn't have any trouble.

JILL: I'll bet you miss him.

DON *(Nodding sadly)*: Very much. He was the only friend I had growing up. He was the kind of man who would have been my friend even if he hadn't been my father. You know what I mean. But it's been rough on Mom since he died because Mom felt she had to be mother *and* father . . . and sister and brother and cousin and uncle and doctor and lawyer . . . Senator . . . Congressman . . .

JILL: I've got it. Why were you born blind? Did the doctor say why?

DON: They said it was a virus in the womb when mother was pregnant—which means they don't know. Whenever they don't know something, they label it "virus."

JILL: I've heard that women with syphilis will give birth to blind babies. Could your mother have had syphilis?

DON: Wait till you meet her, then tell me what *you* think.

JILL: When will I meet her?

DON: In a month. I've got one month before she comes down here to see what's going on. As the clock strikes month, she'll walk in the door. You may have heard of her. She wrote some books. Her name is Florence Baker.

JILL: It's not familiar—but you can't go by me. I could be quoting her and wouldn't know it.

DON: They were a series of children's books. Guess what they were about?

JILL: Children?

DON: A blind kid named Little Donny Dark.

JILL *(Incredulously)*: Little Donny Dark?

DON: That's me.

JILL: Boy, you'll say anything to get attention!

DON: It's true, I swear. I hate that name—Donny. *(He carries the plates toward the centre of the room)* Tell me when to stop.

JILL: Stop. *(DON stops at the edge of the cloth, kneels, and sets the plates down. He sits with his legs crossed under him. JILL gets up)* Just a minute.

DON: Where are you going?

JILL: You'll see. *(She rushes out the front door, and returns a moment later with a small basket of flowers which she offers to* DON *to smell. He smiles.* JILL *places the flowers in the centre of the picnic, stretches out on her stomach and digs into the food)* Tell me about Little Donny Dark. It might curb my appetite.

DON: Donny is twelve years old and was born blind like me, only it's no handicap to Little Donny Dark. He can drive cars and fly planes, 'cause, you see, his other faculties are so highly developed that he can hear a bank being robbed a mile away and he can smell the Communists cooking up a plot to overthrow the government. He's a diligent fighter of crime and injustice, and at the end of every book, as he is being given a medal from the police or the C.I.A. or the F.B.I., he always says, "There are none so blind as those who will not see!"

JILL: I didn't know the police and the F.B.I. gave out medals.

DON: They give 'em to Little Donny Dark. They'd better!

JILL: Boy! Let's have a drink.

DON *(Rising)*: I've only got wine.

JILL: That's all I drink.

DON: With bologna?

JILL: With everything.

(DON *crosses to the chest, passing behind the sofa)*

JILL: Do children really read those books?

DON *(Stopping)*: Shh! I'm counting—so I don't step in the picnic when I come back. (DON *continues to the chest, takes a bottle of wine which has been opened, and some glasses.* JILL *watches, in awe, as he returns and stops, precisely at the edge of the cloth)* Nine steps.

(He sits, placing the bottle and glasses on the cloth. JILL *pours the wine)*

JILL: I could never do that. I'd wind up with both feet in the coleslaw.

DON: No, you wouldn't.

JILL: I speak from experience. Did you ever play Pin the Tail on the Donkey?

DON: I've heard of it.

JILL: We always played it at birthday parties when I was a kid. I remember Julie Patterson's birthday. I guess I was about seven. I was blindfolded and started for the donkey, and stuck the pin smack into Mrs. Patterson's ass.

DON: Well, donkey . . . ass, it's all the same, isn't it?

JILL: Not to Mrs. Patterson it wasn't. She never believed I didn't do it on purpose. I didn't. I didn't have to. I mean if you knew Mrs. Patterson's ass—well, you couldn't miss it—just no way. But *you'd've* won every prize there. My language gets a little raunchy sometimes. I hope you don't mind four-letter words like "ass." *(She takes a long swig of wine)* I'm ready for more.

DON: More what?

JILL: Little Donny Dark. Is she still writing them?

DON: No. She wrote about six. They were pretty popular—no Mary Poppins, but pretty popular . . . *(Wryly)* Unless you happened to be blind. They didn't exactly tell it like it is.

JILL *(Takes a slice of meat from* DON's *plate, having finished her own)*: I'm taking some of your bologna.

DON: I guess the books were sort of a projection of what my mother hoped I'd be—a sightless superman.

JILL: Where did you go to school?

DON: In the living room. I was taught by tutors who teach the blind.

JILL: I thought there were schools for blind children.

DON: There are, but I didn't know that. I didn't know much of anything until about a year ago.

JILL *(Spears a piece of* DON's *bologna with her fork)*: You've just finished your bologna. What happened a year ago?

DON *(Rising)*: A family named Fletcher moved near us and their daughter, Linda, used to come by to read to me. She was the first friend I had after my father died. She was great—a swinger. She used to drive me down here and introduce me to people to take me to parties. All of a sudden, I was living—and learning. At home I was like a pet in a cage. Linda gave me something nobody ever thought to give me—confidence. She talked me into making the break and she found this place for me. At first I was scared to death, but I did it. Maybe it was a mistake . . . I don't know.

JILL *(Rising)*: No, it wasn't. You've got to do it sometime. Your mother isn't going to live forever.

DON: Don't tell her that.

JILL: God, look at someone like Helen Keller. She was blind and deaf and dumb, but she became . . . Helen Keller. What became of Linda?

DON: She got married a few weeks ago and she's living in Chicago. I wish she were here. It would be a lot easier.

JILL: Well, listen, I'm here. I'm right next door. Any time you need me, just knock. You don't even have to knock. Just whisper and I can hear you. *(She looks over at her door)* Hey—you know what?

DON: What?

JILL *(Jumping up)*: Why don't we open that door?

DON: Which door?

JILL: That door to my apartment. There must be a key for it. Let's unlock it. Then we can go back and forth without going out in the hall.

DON: The super probably has a key, but I don't think we ought to ask him. No, I don't think we ought to do that.

JILL: Why not? We're friends, aren't we?

DON: But we'd be practically living together. How would it look? *(Excitedly, answering his own question)* Who cares how it looks? I can't see, anyway!

JILL *(She goes to the kitchen, finds a sharp knife, and returns to her door)*: I'll bet we can open it with this big knife.

DON: We'll have to move the chest.
   (They grab the edges of the chest)

JILL: Move it toward you. *(They move the chest away from the door)* That's fine.
   (JILL sets her end of the chest down and rushes at the lock with the knife. She maneuvers it around, but nothing happens)

DON: What's on the other side?

JILL: My bedroom. This isn't working. Boy, a burglar can just smile at a lock and it opens, but honest people like you and me . . . Tsk!

DON: I heard something click.

JILL: That was me. I went "tsk!" Damn! Maybe we'd better call the super.

DON: Let me try. *(JILL places the knife in* DON's *hand. He feels for the lock and maneuvers the knife around in it, then takes the knife from the lock and delicately works it between the door and the lock)* I felt something.
   (JILL tries the door. It opens)

JILL: You did it! It's open! *(We can see part of* JILL's *bedroom with a lot of her things strewn about untidily. She closes the door quickly, embarrassed)* Oh, don't look! It's an absolute pigsty!

DON *(Covering his eyes and turning away)*: I won't.

JILL *(Sinking)*: I'm sorry.

DON: Stop being sorry.

JILL: I'll get the hang of it. I just don't know when.

>(DON *tries the door to see which way it opens. It opens into* JILL's *apartment)*

JILL: Let's leave it open.

DON *(Going to the kitchen to put the knife away)*: Tell me if you close the door so I won't break my nose on it.

>(JILL *perches on the back of the sofa)*

JILL: Do you wish it were Linda living there instead of me?

DON: I never even thought about it. Why do you ask?

JILL: I was wondering if you're still in love with her.

DON: Did I say I was in love with her?

JILL: If I get too personal, just tell me to shut up. I get carried away. Were you in love with her? Are you?

DON: Every man should have some mystery about him. That'll be mine.

JILL: What's she like?

DON: She's very pretty.

JILL: How do you know?

DON: I can feel someone's face and get a good idea of what they look like. I can tell from shapes and textures.

JILL: Do you wonder what I look like?

DON: Yes.

JILL: I'm gorgeous.

DON: Really?

JILL: I wouldn't lie about something like that.

DON: You know, I've always thought if I could see for just half a minute I'd like to see how I look.

JILL: I'll tell you. Cute . . . and very sexy.

>(DON *smiles and reaches a hand toward* JILL's *face. She takes his hand and places it on her cheek. Gently, he runs his finger up the side of her face, exploring. He runs his hand over the top of her head and takes hold of her long hair, lightly pulling it through his fingers)*

DON: Your hair is very soft . . . and very long. *(Suddenly,* JILL's *long hair—which is really a fall—comes off in* DON's *hand, revealing her own short hair underneath.* DON *is startled as he feels the limp hair in his hand)* Oh, Jesus!

>(He falls back on the sofa)

JILL: Don't be frightened.

DON *(Dropping the fall like a hot potato)*: What happened?

>(JILL *picks up the fall and sits beside him)*

JILL: It's a fall. It's a piece of long hair that you attach to your head.

DON: It's not *your* hair?

JILL: It's not even my fall. I borrowed it from Susan Potter. I do have hair of my own. See? I mean, feel?

>(She places his hand on her head. DON *takes in the shape of her head, then moves his hand along her face, over her eyes. A false eyelash comes off in his hand)*

DON: God! Now what?

JILL *(Takes the eyelash from him and puts it back on)*: That's just a false eyelash.

DON: Don't you have eyelashes?

JILL: Of course, but these make your eyes look bigger. They're longer than mine. Didn't Linda wear them?

DON: No.

JILL: She probably has naturally long lashes. I hate her. *(Placing his hand on her cheek)* Go on.

DON: This is scaring the hell out of me.

JILL: It's all right. Everything's real from now on. *(DON runs his fingers across JILL's mouth)* Am I not the image of Elizabeth Taylor.

DON: I've never felt Elizabeth Taylor.

JILL: We look exactly alike. Especially if you can't see.

> *(JILL smiles at DON, oddly, as his fingers explore her throat. She takes his hand and leans down to kiss him again. DON twists his head away from her, suddenly, anguished)* What's the matter?

DON: What do you think is the matter?

JILL: If I knew I wouldn't ask.

DON: Why are you doing this? Is it "Be Kind to the Handicapped Week" or something? *(Raising himself on one elbow)* Don't patronize me! And don't feel sorry for me!

JILL *(Hotly)*: I'm doing it because I want to do it! And I'll be goddamned if I feel sorry for any guy who's going to have sex with me!

> *(DON's hand is on her shoulder now. The lights fade, slowly. The curtain is lowered to denote the passing of a few hours. We can hear DON playing the guitar and singing: "On that velvet morning/When our love was forming/I said it wouldn't hurt me/if you left without warning/I said, 'Butterflies are free/And so are we' ")*

SCENE TWO

When the curtain rises the remnants of the picnic lunch are still on the floor. JILL's blouse and jeans lie in a heap nearby. Her fall is on the coffee table. DON's shirt and trousers are hanging over the back of a chair. DON, dressed only in his jockey shorts, is on the sofa, playing his guitar and singing. JILL calls from her apartment.

JILL *(Offstage)*: I can't find it. I can't find anything in this mess.

DON: What are you looking for?

JILL *(Offstage)*: Never mind. It's here somewhere.

> (DON *continues to play.* JILL *enters from her apartment, dressed only in panties and bra, and carrying a box a little larger than a cigar box, made of beautiful wood and mother-of-pearl. She curls up on the sofa beside* DON)

JILL: I found it.

DON: What is it?

JILL: My secret box. I take it with me everywhere. Here. Feel it.

> (JILL *places* DON's *hand on the box. He runs his fingers over it)*

DON: Beautiful wood.

JILL: And mother-of-pearl.

DON *(Smiling)*: What do you keep in it?

JILL: *(Opening the box and rummaging through it)*: Everything important to me. *(She takes out a small piece of rock)* This is a piece of the moon or a star. *(She places it in* DON's *hand)* I found it in the desert. I showed it to a geologist who said he'd never seen any mineral like it on earth, and it probably fell here from the moon or maybe a star.

DON: It feels like a rock.

JILL *(Taking it and putting it back in the box)*: I know, but it isn't. *(She takes out a baby tooth and holds it up)* One of my baby teeth. *(She puts the tooth back and rummages through some papers)* My birth certificate . . . A picture of me when I was in *The Mikado* in high school. It's not very good anyway . . . my last will and testament.

DON: Your last will and testament?

JILL: *(Holding up a sheet of yellow foolscap paper)*: And the instructions for my funeral. My entire estate is to be divided, equally, among whoever are my four closest friends when I die. Names to be filled in later.

DON: I thought you didn't like anything morbid.

JILL: But that's the point. It isn't morbid. Funerals don't have to be morbid. I want mine in a large church, but I want all the pews and seats removed and just lots of big cushions for people to lie on. I don't want anyone dressed in black. They should all be in gay, bright colours and far-out clothes and they should all be drinking or smoking pot or whatever they like. I want Salvador Dali to paint the walls with lots of groovy pictures and I want tons of flowers, but not formal wreaths. Just tons of wild flowers strewn everywhere.

DON: Butterflies?

JILL: Oh, yes, lots of butterflies. And I want music going all the time. I want the Beatles to write a special memoriam for me and to sing it. And I want the Rolling Stones to sing and Simon and Garfunkle and the Doors and the Vienna Boys' Choir.

DON: And me . . .

JILL: . . . and you . . .

DON: How about a eulogy?

JILL: Yes—to be delivered by Sidney Poitier. I love his voice. And at the same time I want André Previn playing "Ave Maria" on the organ. If he can't come, maybe Leonard Bernstein. There's nothing morbid about that, is there?

DON: Not at all.

JILL *(Taking some hippie beads from the box)*: Oh, here it is! A present for you.
(She slips the beads over his neck)

DON: What is it?

JILL: What does it feel like?

DON: A necklace.

JILL: They're love beads. I wore them when I was a hippie. You ought to wear beads if you're going to play the guitar.

DON: Nobody told me.

JILL: Donovan wears them . . . and Jimi Hendrix.

DON: What else should I wear?

JILL *(Rising as she studies him)*: Oh, some kicky clothes—wild. And your hair doesn't exactly blow the mind.

DON: What's wrong with it?

JILL: I can fix it.
(She runs into her apartment)

DON: What's wrong with it?

JILL *(Offstage)*: The way you comb it.
(JILL returns, carrying her purse, and looking through it)

JILL: It's a little square. I can fix it. I know I have a comb here. *(She looks toward the kitchen)* Is there anything left to eat? I'm starving.

DON: So soon?

JILL: Isn't it awful?

DON: There should be a couple of apples.
(JILL tucks the purse under her arm and rushes to the refrigerator. She opens it and peers in)

JILL: There's an awful lot of lettuce—which is not exactly what I was dreaming of. I only see one apple.
(She takes the apple out)

DON: It's yours.

JILL: Thanks. *(She returns to the sofa with the apple in her mouth, and searches through her purse. She produces a comb and a small pair of scissors. When she runs the comb through DON's hair, he is startled)* Just sit still. I'm very good at this.

DON: I don't know that I want to look like a hippie.

JILL: You're not going to look like a hippie. You're going to look hip.
(She settles on the sofa arm and proceeds to do his hair over, combing it forward and snipping at it as she eats her apple)

DON: When were you a hippie?

JILL: I guess it was right after my marriage. I used to hang around the Sunset Strip and smoke pot and say things like "Down with the fuzz" and "Don't trust anyone over thirty." The whole bit. I just did it because everybody was doing it. Then I stopped because everybody was doing it. I felt I was losing my individuality— whatever that is. The main thing, of course, was to protest against my mother, but it didn't work. I mean I walked in one day with my hair long and stringy, wearing far-out clothes and beads and sandals . . . and she LOVED it! Next day, *she* had stringy hair and far-out clothes and beads and sandals. Well, I mean how can you protest against someone who's doing the same thing you are? Right? So, I went the other way and joined the Young Republicans for Ronald Reagan. Another mistake. There's no such thing as a young Republican. *(She finishes with his hair and studies it)* There. You look terrific.

(Without thinking, she takes a small mirror from her bag and holds it up in front of his face. Realizing her mistake, she makes a face to herself and slips the mirror back into her bag)

DON: It doesn't look too wild, does it?

JILL: I think it looks great. It gives you charisma.

DON: What do you mean—charisma?

JILL: It's like pizazz. Star quality. It's better than talent. If you have charisma you don't need anything else. They'll line up for blocks to see you. *(She looks at him for a moment, then kisses him, gently, on the lips)* You're beautiful, you know? I mean you're a beautiful person inside as well as out.

DON *(Smiling)*: I like you, too.

JILL: I feel I ought to tell you something.

DON: What?

JILL: Well, before . . . when I took your hand and put it on me . . . were you shocked?

DON: Sort of. I don't mean from the standpoint of morals or anything. I was just surprised to be feeling something when I wasn't expecting to.

JILL: I wouldn't like you to think that I go around putting men's hands on me.

DON: No, I don't think you go around doing that.

JILL: If I want to be with a guy . . . usually I have a little smile that lets him know I'm interested.

DON *(Reaching his hand out)*: Smile that smile. I want to feel it.

JILL *(Tries her come-hither smile, but starts to giggle helplessly)*: I can't. You're making me laugh.

DON *(Running his fingers across her laughing mouth)*: Is that it?

JILL: No, of course not. Oh, I can't do it now. I'll do it later. But I had to use a different approach with you, didn't I? Well, I didn't want you to think I was terrible.

DON: I didn't. I don't.

JILL: I hate talking about sex, but I thought maybe you'd like to know that you're . . . well, really groovy.

DON *(Smiling)*: Like the Fourth of July?

JILL: Like the Fourth of July—and like Christmas.

DON: Where are you going?

JILL: I'm going to throw the apple core away—and maybe I'll have some lettuce.

As JILL *crosses to the kitchen to throw away the apple core,* DON *rises and starts up the ladder to his bed. The door opens quietly and* MRS. BAKER *enters. She is an attractive, well-dressed woman, carrying a Saks Fifth Avenue box. She smiles at* DON *silently.* JILL, *in an effort to hide her near-nudity, bumps into a waste basket noisily.* MRS. BAKER *turns to look at her for a moment; she completes the turn, looking back at* DON *with disapproval.* DON *sits on his bed, aware of someone new in the room).*

DON *(Sagging)*: Hello, Mother!

(Blackout)

Curtain

Act Two

SCENE ONE

The scene is the same, a moment later. DON *is sitting on the sofa, gritting his teeth and trying not to show his annoyance.* JILL *is still peeking out from behind the shutters.* MRS. BAKER *closes the door behind her.*

MRS. BAKER: I'm glad I found you in, Donny.
DON: Jill, this is my mother.
JILL: Your mother? Have I been here a month?
DON: Mother, this is . . . Mrs. Benson.
> (MRS. BAKER *studies* JILL *from head to toe with ill-concealed disapproval)*
JILL: How do you do?
MRS. BAKER *(Coolly)*: How do you do, Mrs. Benson? Are you living here, too?
JILL: I live next door. I just stopped in to ask Don to . . . er . . . I had trouble zipping up my blouse.
MRS. BAKER: So I see. Where *is* your blouse?
JILL *(Looking around)*: It's here somewhere. *(She sees it on the floor and rushes to get it)* There it is. You see I have this long zipper in the back. It's hard to do alone.
> (Jill *scrambles into her blouse.* MRS. BAKER *picks up* DON's *clothes and places them on his lap)*
MRS. BAKER: Put your things on.
DON *(Rises and dresses)*: All right, Mom, what are you doing here? We had an agreement.
MRS. BAKER: I was in the neighbourhood . . .
DON: You were at Saks, which is on 50th Street and Fifth Avenue. This is 11th Street between Second and Third.
MRS. BAKER: I bought you some shirts, and I thought you'd have them sooner if I brought them myself.
DON: I don't need any shirts. You just brought them as an excuse to come down here.
> (JILL *goes to* MRS. BAKER *and turns her back to be zipped)*
JILL: Would you mind?
> (MRS. BAKER *glares daggers at* JILL's *back, but zips up the blouse as she looks around the room)*
MRS. BAKER: And this is what you left home for?
DON: This is it.
MRS. BAKER: It isn't Buckingham Palace, is it?
DON: No, it's the Taj Mahal.
> (MRS. BAKER *moves around, stopping to look at the "picnic" things on the floor)*

MRS. BAKER: Is this where you eat—on the floor?

DON: It's fun eating on the floor, Mom. You ought to try it.

    (A withering glance from MRS. BAKER *is* DON's *reply.* MRS. BAKER *takes in the sofa and chairs)*

MRS. BAKER: Where did this furniture come from?

DON: Some of it came with the apartment and some of it I picked up in a junk shop.

MRS. BAKER: Don't tell me which is which. Let me guess. *(*MRS. BAKER *goes to* JILL's *door and looks inside, in disbelief)* What in God's name is this?

DON: I don't know what you're looking at.

JILL: That's my apartment.

MRS. BAKER: Have you ever thought about hiring a maid, Mrs. Benson?

JILL: I can manage. I may be sloppy, but I'm not dirty. There's a difference between sloppy and dirty.

MRS. BAKER: I'm so glad to hear that.

DON: So she's not Craig's wife.

MRS. BAKER: Has this door always been open?

DON: No, it's always been locked. I opened it this morning.

MRS. BAKER: What on earth *is* that?

DON: Now what are you looking at?

MRS. BAKER: That's what I'd like to know.

JILL: It's your bed.

DON: My bed.

JILL: Isn't that wonderful?

MRS. BAKER *(Looking the bed over, incredulously)*: You actually sleep up there?

DON: Like a baby.

MRS. BAKER: What happens if you fall out?

DON: I go to the ladder and climb up again.

MRS. BAKER: Where are your clothes?

DON: There's a closet and chest in the bathroom.

MRS. BAKER: And where is the bathroom—under the bed?

DON: That's right.

MRS. BAKER: Of course it is.

    *(*MRS. BAKER *exits to the bathroom.* JILL *rushes to* DON*)*

JILL: Boy, were you ever right!

DON: About what?

JILL: She never had syphilis. I'm surprised she had you. Why did you introduce me as Mrs. Benson?

DON: I don't know. It makes you sound . . . more important.

    (Offstage we can hear the sound of the toilet flushing)

JILL: What is she doing?

DON: Testing the plumbing. She's a nut about plumbing.

JILL: Sssh! How did you know it was your mother when she came in? She didn't make a sound.

DON *(Sniffing the air)*: Smell. (JILL *sniffs the air)* It's called Numéro Dix and she uses half a bottle at a time. I always know when she's around.

JILL: It's like having a bell on a cat. *(Offstage we hear the sound of drawers opening and closing)* Now what is she doing?

DON: Checking the drawers to see if I have enough socks and underwear. She's a nut about socks and underwear. What she's really doing is gathering up evidence to hit me with and try to make me come home. I was so sure she'd walk in and say, "I could absolutely cry." She let me down.

JILL: She's not finished. She'll say it.

DON: No, she'd have said it by now. I know all her routines.

JILL: What do you want to bet she says it? How about dinner tonight? If she doesn't say it, we eat in my place and I pay. If she says it, we eat here and you pay.

DON: It's a bet, but you might as well start shopping.

(MRS. BAKER *enters from the bathroom*)

MRS. BAKER: Well, that's some bathroom. No wonder you hide it under the bed.

DON: Gee, I thought you were going to say something else.

MRS. BAKER: I haven't finished. I haven't even started.

DON: Well, say it and get it over with.

MRS. BAKER: Well, there's only one thing *to* say.

JILL *(Aside to* DON*)*: Here it comes.

MRS. BAKER: Perhaps it's a blessing that you can't see what you're living in.

DON: Right, Mom. I count that blessing every time I come in the door.

MRS. BAKER: Donny, can I be honest?

DON: *Can* you?

JILL *(Aside to* DON*)*: This is it.

MRS. BAKER: I am shocked and appalled.

JILL: I lose. Seven-thirty all right?

DON: Perfect.

MRS. BAKER: There's no tub in your bathroom.

DON: It's under the dining table.

MRS. BAKER: I could absolutely cry!

DON *(To* JILL*)*: You win! Hamburgers all right?

JILL: But at least two each.

MRS. BAKER: I am not just talking about this rat hole, Donny. I am talking about you, too. You're so thin. You've lost weight.

DON: I haven't lost anything. I'm exactly the right weight for my height—six-one—and my age—eleven.

MRS. BAKER *(Goes to the refrigerator)*: I'd like to see what you're eating. *(She opens it and looks in, carefully)* There's nothing in here but lettuce . . . and an apple.

JILL: Where?

MRS. BAKER: Behind the lettuce.

DON: I knew there was another one.

(MRS. BAKER *closes the refrigerator and turns back into the room. Her appraising glance falls on* JILL. *She stares at her for a moment;* JILL *grows uncomfortable)*

MRS. BAKER: Tell me, where is *Mr.* Benson?

JILL: Who's Mr. Benson?

MRS. BAKER: I assumed he was your husband.

JILL: Oh, Jack. I don't know. Last time I saw him he was sitting outside of Hamburger Hamlet on the Strip. Why?

MRS. BAKER: I was curious about your marital status.

JILL: I haven't any.

DON: Jill is divorced.

MRS. BAKER: How old are you, Mrs. Benson?

JILL: Nineteen.

MRS. BAKER: Nineteen? And you've already been married and divorced?

JILL: Yeah . . . And now I'm allowed to vote.

MRS. BAKER: I think you should be allowed to run. How long were you married?

JILL: Six days.

MRS. BAKER: And on the seventh day you rested?

JILL: No, I split. I have to change now. I have an audition.

MRS. BAKER: An audition for what?

DON: A play. An off-Broadway play.

MRS. BAKER: I was speaking to Mrs. Benson.

JILL: A play. An off-Broadway play.

MRS. BAKER: Then, you're an actress.

JILL: Well . . . yes.

MRS. BAKER: Might I have seen you in anything—besides your underwear?

JILL: Not unless you went to Beverly Hills High School. I was in *The Mikado*. I played Yum Yum.

MRS. BAKER: Yes, I'm sure you did.

JILL: And about a year ago I did a TV commercial for Panacin.

MRS. BAKER: What is Panacin?

JILL: You know, it's for acid indigestion.

MRS. BAKER: No, I don't know. One of the few problems I *don't* have is acid indigestion.

DON: There are givers and there are takers.

MRS. BAKER: You're asking for it, Donny. *(To* JILL*)* Does your mother know where you are?

JILL: Sure.

MRS. BAKER: And does she approve of the way you're living?

JILL: What "way" am I living?

DON: Mom, are you conducting some kind of survey?

MRS. BAKER: And you're going to get it. I'm sure Mrs. Benson doesn't mind answering a few questions. Do you, Mrs. Benson?

JILL: Well, I have this audition . . .

MRS. BAKER: What does your father do?

JILL: Which one?

MRS. BAKER: How many fathers have you?

JILL: Four. One real and three steps.

MRS. BAKER: Your mother has been married FOUR times?

JILL: So far. We live in Los Angeles.

MRS. BAKER: Then you come from a broken home.

JILL: Several.

MRS. BAKER: Why does your mother marry so often?

JILL: I don't know. I guess she likes it. I mean she likes *getting* married. Obviously, she doesn't like *being* married. I'd better get started. Okay. See you later, Don.

DON: Good luck!

JILL: Thanks

DON: Don't forget—seven-thirty here.

MRS. BAKER: What happens at seven-thirty here?

DON: Jill and I are having dinner together.

MRS. BAKER: Mrs. Benson . . .

DON: Just the two of us. Alone!

MRS. BAKER: Mrs. Benson, I think you've forgotten something. *(As* JILL *turns,* MRS. BAKER *picks up the fall, gingerly, and holds it out to her)*

DON: What is it?

JILL: Susan Potter's hair.

(JILL takes the fall and exits to her apartment, closing the door)

DON: Did you have to be so goddamn rude?

MRS. BAKER: Was I rude?

DON: All those questions! What are you—the Attorney General of Scarsdale?

MRS. BAKER: I think I have a right to know something about my son's friends.

DON: Let's talk about my rights! You're not supposed to be here for another month. Why did you have to come today, huh?

MRS. BAKER: Since when do you speak to me this way?

DON: Since when do you come sneaking into my room this way?

MRS. BAKER: I didn't come sneaking in. The door was unlocked.

DON: You could have knocked. I thought it was a raid.

MRS. BAKER: It should have been. Why don't you lock your door?

DON: Until I knew my way around the room, it was easier to let people come in on their own, but it'll be locked from now on.

MRS. BAKER: I thought my coming here would be a pleasant surprise for you. Had I known I'd be treated like the Long Island Railroad—

DON: You'd've come anyway.

MRS. BAKER: And I'm glad I did. My worst fears have been realized.

DON: Thank heaven! *My* worst fear was that *your* worst fears wouldn't be realized. Can you imagine if you came here and liked it? We'd have nothing to talk about.

MRS. BAKER: Did you have to choose such a sordid neighbourhood?

DON: To me it looks just like Scarsdale.

MRS. BAKER: There are lots of nice places up in the Sixties and Seventies.

DON: I don't trust anybody over 30th Street.

MRS. BAKER: I'd be terrified to live with the type of people down here.

DON: They've been nice to me.

MRS. BAKER *(Glancing at* JILL's *door)*: I'll bet they have. This morning you told me you didn't know Mrs. Benson's name.

DON: I didn't. I hadn't met her when we talked.

MRS. BAKER: You certainly made friends in a hurry, didn't you?

DON: She's a very friendly girl.

MRS. BAKER: I can see she is. May I ask you a personal question?

DON: No.

MRS. BAKER: Have you slept with this girl?

DON: I thought you'd never ask. Yes, I have.

MRS. BAKER: As if I didn't know.

DON: If you know, why did you ask?

MRS. BAKER: And now I know why you're so anxious to have a place of your own. Not because you want to do something constructive with your life. You just want a place where you can have orgies—night and day!

DON: Oh, Mother. Two's company, three's an orgy.

MRS. BAKER: I know you, Donny. You've got that Linda Fletcher look on your face again. You're going to fall in love with this girl, too.

DON: Maybe I will. Does it bother you that I'm heterosexual?

MRS. BAKER: Mrs. Benson is not exactly the sort of girl a mother dreams of for her son.

DON: Mom, I'm not interested in the girl of *your* dreams.

MRS. BAKER: Obviously a stupid girl.

DON: Not at all. She even quotes Dylan Thomas.

MRS. BAKER: How wonderful! I can assure you Dylan Thomas never quoted *her*. And she's not at all attractive.

DON: Oh, come on now—

MRS. BAKER: She has beady little eyes like a bird and a figure like . . . a pogo stick.

DON: You've just described the girl of *my* dreams.

MRS. BAKER: You can't see the difference between good and bad. I can see people's faces. I can see into their eyes. You can't.

DON: Ah, but I can see past their eyes and into their souls. Leave us not forget Little Donny Dark and all that vision.

MRS. BAKER: You don't know what you're talking about. You've never been exposed to life.

DON: Whose fault is that? Whose fault is it I didn't go to school with other kids?

MRS. BAKER: How could you?

DON: There are schools for blind kids.

MRS. BAKER: We could afford to have you taught at home. I thought that was better than sending you off with a bunch of blind children like . . . a leper.

DON: Is that how you see me—like a leper?

MRS. BAKER: Of course not!

DON: Come on, Mom, deep, deep down haven't you always been just a little ashamed that you produced a blind child?

MRS. BAKER: It's nothing to be ashamed of.

DON: Embarrassed, then.

MRS. BAKER: You have never given me reason to be embarrassed by you.

    (There is a knock at JILL's *door)*

DON: Come in.

    (JILL enters in a different outfit. She crosses to MRS. BAKER *and turns her unzipped back to her)*

JILL: I hate to bother you.

    *(*MRS. BAKER *zips it up in one contemptuous zip)*

DON: What's wrong?

JILL: Just another zipper. *(She starts toward her door, stopping to whisper to* DON*)* I think you're winning. Hang in there! *(To* MRS. BAKER, *sweetly)* Thank you.

    (JILL exits to her apartment, closing the door)

MRS. BAKER: She'll be a great help to you. She can't even dress herself.

DON: That's where I can help her.

    *(*MRS. BAKER *has been looking at the bed with interest; she turns to* DON *enthusiastically)*

MRS. BAKER: Donny, I have a wonderful idea! You come on home. I'll have your bed raised—and there's a ladder in the garage. I'll put up some psychedelic posters . . .

DON: Nice try, Mother, but it just wouldn't be the same.

MRS. BAKER: All right! If you insist on staying here, I will not support you.

    (DON rushes to the telephone and picks it up)

MRS. BAKER: What are you doing?

DON: Calling *The Daily News.* What a story! "Florence Baker refuses to help the handicapped!"

MRS. BAKER *(Grabbing the phone away)*: I'm serious, Donny!

DON: Oh, then I'll call *The Times.*

MRS. BAKER: What are you going to do for money? The little you saved must be gone now.

DON: I have some left.

MRS. BAKER: And when that's gone?

DON: I can always walk along the street with a tin cup.

MRS. BAKER: Now, you *are* embarrassing me.

DON: Don't worry, Mom. I'll keep away from Saks.

MRS. BAKER: Just stop all this joking. I want to know what your plans are.

DON: I'm going to sing and play the guitar. I'm pretty good. You've said so yourself.

MRS. BAKER: I didn't know you were planning to make a career of it. Have you any idea of the competition you're facing?

DON: I have just as good a chance as anyone else. Better. I have charisma.

MRS. BAKER: May I ask how you arrived at this brilliant decision?

DON: It was elementary, my dear mother—by the process of elimination. I made a lengthy list of all the things I could *not* do, like, well, like commercial pilot. I don't think TWA would be too thrilled to have me fly their planes, nor United, nor Pan Am. Photographer? A definite out—along with ball player and cab driver. Matador didn't strike me as too promising. I half considered becoming an eye doctor, but that would just be a case of the blind leading the blind. That's a little joke. *(Shrugs when he gets no response)* I said it was little.

MRS. BAKER: I suppose Linda Fletcher put this guitar idea into your head.

DON: You might say she was instrumental. *(Waits for a response to this)* That was another joke, Mom. You'd better start laughing at something or people will think you're a lesbian.

MRS. BAKER: You've certainly picked up some colourful language, haven't you?

DON: You can learn anything down here.

MRS. BAKER *(Goes to the bathroom door)*: Yes. Well, I think you've learned enough, young man. I hardly recognize my own son.

> *(She enters the bathroom and brings out a suitcase)*

DON: What are you doing?

MRS. BAKER *(Plunks the suitcase down loudly on a chair)*: I'm doing what I should have done long ago. I'm taking you home.

DON: Forget it, Mother. There's no way—

MRS. BAKER: You cannot stay here alone!

DON: I'm not alone. I have friends.

MRS. BAKER: Oh, don't think you've fooled me with all your parties. There are no parties! You have no friends!

DON: I have now. I have Mrs. Benson.

MRS. BAKER: You'd be better off with a seeing-eye dog.

DON: They're not as much fun. Anyway, I've got a seeing-eye mother.

MRS. BAKER *(Snapping open the suitcase)*: That's right—and she's taking you home. Mrs. Benson will just have to learn to dress herself.

DON: Put that suitcase away!

MRS. BAKER: You're coming home, Donny!

DON *(Firmly)*: Give me that suitcase! (DON *lunges across to the chair where he heard the suitcase placed.* MRS. BAKER *lifts the suitcase from the chair.* DON

stumbles around trying to find the suitcase) Where is it? Give me that suitcase, Mother! *(He stands, holding his hand out)* Give it to me! *(*MRS. BAKER *stands staring at* DON *for a moment, as iron-willed as he. Suddenly, a wave of resignation comes over her. She takes* DON's *hand and places it on the suitcase handle.* DON *grabs the handle, carries the suitcase to the bathroom, opens the door, throws the bag in, and closes the door. His tension ebbs and he goes over to his mother)* Mom, please stop worrying about me. I'm going to be all right. If the music doesn't work out, I can always study law or technology. There are lots of things blind people can do now. So, don't worry any more. *(He reaches his hand out to find her.* MRS. BAKER *takes his hand and places it on her face.* DON *kisses her cheek)* Well, I have to go, Mom. Thanks for dropping by.
　　　(He crosses to his jacket and walking stick)
MRS. BAKER: Where are you going?
DON: I have to do some shopping. I told you, I'm having dinner in tonight . . . with Mrs. Benson . . . just the two of us—*alone.*
MRS. BAKER: I'll wait till you come back.
DON: I don't want you to wait. Have a nice trip back to Scarsdale and I'll call you tomorrow. Now, please. I don't want to smell you here when I get back.
MRS. BAKER: I was planning to stay for dinner.
DON: Your plans have changed. Like I said, it's me and Mrs. Benson, just the two of us—*alone.*
MRS. BAKER: And after dinner, I suppose an orgy.
DON *(Opening the front door)*: I hope so. At last the sinister truth is revealed—Little Donny Dark is just a dirty old man!
　　　*(*DON *makes a clicking sound, winks and exits.* MRS. BAKER *looks around the room with frustration. She goes over to the picnic lunch, picks up the dishes, puts them on a tray, carries them to the kitchen and sets them down)*
MRS. BAKER *(Mumbling to herself)*: Mrs. Benson!
JILL *(Opening her door)*: Yes?
　　　*(*MRS. BAKER *is startled for a moment, but recovers quickly)*
MRS. BAKER *(In sweet, dulcet tones)*: Could you come in for a moment, Mrs. Benson?
JILL *(Uneasily)*: Well, I have my audition. I should leave in about fifteen minutes. I don't know New York and I get lost all the time.
MRS. BAKER *(Ingratiatingly)*: Don't you worry. I'll see that you get off in time. *(*JILL *enters, reluctantly)* I thought you and I might have a little talk. You know, just girls together. Please sit down. *(*JILL *remains standing, avoiding too-close contact with* MRS. BAKER*)* Would you like a cup of coffee? tea?
JILL: No, thank you. But if that apple is still there . . .
MRS. BAKER: I'm sure it is.
JILL: Where's Don?
MRS. BAKER *(Opening the refrigerator and taking out the apple)*: Shopping. *(She washes the apple in the sink, and polishes it with a dishtowel)* You must be so careful to wash fruits and vegetables, you know. They spray all those insecticides on everything now. I'm not at all sure the bugs aren't less harmful. I like apples to be nice and shiny.
　　　*(*MRS. BAKER *holds the apple out to* JILL, *who looks at it and then at* MRS. BAKER, *oddly)*
JILL: This reminds me of something. What is it?

MRS. BAKER: I have no idea.

JILL: You . . . handing me the apple . . . nice and shiny . . . Oh, I know! Snow White. Remember when the witch brought her the poisoned apple? I'm sorry. I didn't mean that the way it sounded. I know you're not a witch.

MRS. BAKER: Of course not. And I know you're not Snow White.

(JILL *takes the apple*)

JILL: I may have to wait hours before I read. I'll probably starve to death before their eyes.

MRS. BAKER: You're going to get that part, you know.

JILL: What makes you so sure?

MRS. BAKER: Well, you're a very pretty girl and that's what they want in the theatre, isn't it?

JILL: Today you have to have more than a pretty face. Anyway, I'm not really pretty. I think I'm interesting-looking, and in certain lights I can look sort of . . . lovely, but I'm not pretty.

MRS. BAKER: Nonsense! You're extremely pretty.

JILL *(Laughs)*: No, I'm not.

MRS. BAKER: Yes, you *are*.

JILL: No, I'm not. I've got beady little eyes like a bird, and a figure like a pogo stick. *(She waits for a reaction from* MRS. BAKER. *There isn't one)*: Well? Aren't you going to deny you said that?

MRS. BAKER *(Unperturbed)*: How can I, dear? Obviously, you heard it.

JILL: There are plenty of true things you can put me down with. You don't have to put me down with lies.

MRS. BAKER: You know what I like about you?

JILL: Nothing.

MRS. BAKER: Oh, yes. I like your honesty . . . your candor. You're really quite a wordly young woman, aren't you, Mrs. Benson?

JILL: I suppose I am. I wish you wouldn't call me Mrs. Benson.

MRS. BAKER: That's your name, isn't it? Mrs. Benson?

JILL: But you don't say it as though you mean it.

MRS. BAKER: I'm sorry. Why don't I call you Jill? That's more friendly—and I'll try to say it as though I mean it. Now, Jill, you were telling me about your childhood.

JILL: I was?

MRS. BAKER: It must have been interesting having so many fathers.

JILL: Well, it was, actually. All mother's husbands were so different, so I was exposed to all kinds of ideas about life, and world affairs—even religion. My real father was a Methodist. My next father was a Christian Scientist. The next was Jewish and the last one was Episcopalian.

MRS. BAKER: That covers just about everything. Doesn't your mother like Catholics?

JILL: Oh, yes, she likes them, but for some reason Catholics are not allowed to marry her.

MRS. BAKER: I would imagine she's got an X-rating from the church.

JILL: Too bad. She's really very nice.

MRS. BAKER: I'm sure she is. So it's your childhood that has made you so worldly and understanding.

JILL: Yes, and being so worldly and understanding, Mrs. Baker, I can tell that you didn't ask me here to discuss my childhood or to tell me how pretty I am.

MRS. BAKER: I was interested in seeing what you and Donny might have in common. He likes you very much.

JILL: And I like him very much. He may very well be the most beautiful person I've ever met. Just imagine going through life never seeing anything . . . not a painting, or a flower, or even a Christmas card. I'd want to die, but Don wants to live. I mean really *live*. And he can even kid about it. He's fantastic.

MRS. BAKER: Then you would want what's best for him, wouldn't you?

JILL: Now we're getting to it, aren't we? Like maybe I should tell him to go home with you. Is that it?

MRS. BAKER: Donny was happy at home until Linda Fletcher filled him with ideas about a place of his own.

JILL: Maybe you just want to believe that he can only be happy with you, Mrs. Baker. Well, "There are none so blind as those who will not see." There. I can quote Dylan Thomas AND Little Donny Dark.

MRS. BAKER: You constantly astonish me.

JILL: Well, we women of the world do that.

MRS. BAKER: Funny how like Linda you are. Donny is certainly consistent with his girls.

JILL: Why do you call him Donny?

MRS. BAKER: It's his name. Don't I say it as though I mean it?

JILL: He hates being called Donny.

MRS. BAKER: He's never mentioned it.

JILL: Of course, he has. You just didn't listen. There are none so deaf as those who will not hear. You could make up a lot of those, couldn't you? There are none so lame as those who will not walk. None so thin as those who will not eat—

MRS. BAKER: Do you think it's a good idea for Donny to live down here alone?

JILL: I think it's a good idea for *Don* to live wherever he wants to . . . and he's not alone. I'm here.

MRS. BAKER: For how long? Have you got a lease on that apartment?

JILL: No.

MRS. BAKER: So, you can leave tomorrow if you felt like it.

JILL: That's right.

MRS. BAKER: You couldn't sustain a marriage for more than six days, could you?

JILL *(Upset)*: My marriage doesn't concern you.

MRS. BAKER: It didn't concern you much, either, did it?

JILL: Yes, it did!

MRS. BAKER: Have you thought about what marriage to a blind boy might be like? Let's face it, not even your mother has covered THAT territory!

JILL: Suppose we leave my mother out of this, huh?

MRS. BAKER: I'm sorry. I didn't know you were so touchy about her.

JILL: I'm not touchy about her. I just don't want to talk about her.

MRS. BAKER: All right. We'll talk about you. Look, Jill, you've seen Donny at his best—in this room, which he's memorized. And he's memorized how many steps to the drugstore, and to the delicatessen. But take him out of this room or off this street and he's lost; he panics. Donny needs someone who will stay with him—and not just for six days.

JILL: You can stop worrying, Mrs. Baker. Nothing serious will develop between Don and me. I'm not built that way!

MRS. BAKER: But Donny *is* built that way.

JILL: Oh, please—we're just having kicks.

MRS. BAKER: Kicks! That's how it started with Linda—just kicks. But Donny fell in love with her . . . and he'll fall in love with you. Then what happens?

JILL: I don't know!

MRS. BAKER: Then don't let it go that far. Stop it now before you hurt him.

JILL: What about you? Aren't you hurting him?

MRS. BAKER: I can't. I can only irritate him. You can hurt him. The longer you stay, the harder it will be for him when you leave. Let him come with me and you go have your kicks with someone who won't feel them after you've gone!

(JILL *turns to face* MRS. BAKER, *studying her intently*)

JILL: I'm not so sure you can't hurt him. Maybe more than anybody. I think you deserve all the credit you can get for turning out a pretty marvelous guy. But bringing up a son—even a blind one—isn't a lifetime occupation. Now the more you help him, the more you hurt him. It was Linda Fletcher—not you—who gave him the thing he needed most: confidence in himself. You're always dwelling on the negative—always what he needs, never what he wants; always what he can't do, never what he can. What about his music? Have you heard the song he wrote? I'll bet you didn't even know he could write songs! You're probably dead right about me. I'm not the ideal girl for Don, but I know one thing—neither are you! And if I'm going to tell anyone to go home, it'll be you, Mrs. Baker. YOU go home!

(JILL *turns*)

Curtain

SCENE TWO

The scene is the same, that night. The dining table is set for two, with JILL's *basket of flowers and some lighted votive candles on it.* DON *is adjusting the silverware on the table.* MRS. BAKER *is in the kitchen, noisily looking through a cabinet.*

DON: Oh, Mom, what are you doing in there?

MRS. BAKER: I'm looking for some wax paper to wrap the meat in so it doesn't spoil.

DON: I haven't any wax paper and the meat won't spoil.

MRS. BAKER: This meat looks terrible.

DON: Who asked you to look at it. Why don't you get out of the kitchen?

MRS. BAKER: What time is it? Midnight?

DON *(Feeling his braille watch)*: It's only twenty to ten.

MRS. BAKER: *Only* twenty to ten?

DON: I know. She's undependable and unreliable. She's uneverything. What else is new?

MRS. BAKER: You did say seven-thirty. I heard you.

DON: Listen, you don't have to hang around, you know.

MRS. BAKER: I'll just wait until she comes. *(Going to the tape recorder)* I'm not going to interfere with your orgy. I told you that.

DON: No, I told you that. (MRS. BAKER *turns the tape recorder on.* DON's *singing and playing of "Butterflies Are Free" is heard.* MRS. BAKER *listens, impressed. Moving toward* JILL's *door)* Mom, please turn it off. I want to hear if she comes in.

MRS. BAKER: Is that the song you wrote?

DON: Yes . . . well, it's not finished. *(Thinks for a second)* How'd you know I wrote it?

MRS. BAKER: I didn't. I just asked you.

DON: Oh.

MRS. BAKER: It's good. Pretty.

DON: You mean pretty good?

MRS. BAKER: No, I mean good and pretty.

DON: Wow.

      (DON *turns toward his mother with some surprise as he moves away from* JILL's *door)*

MRS. BAKER: Where do you suppose she is?

DON: Probably still auditioning.

MRS. BAKER: For six hours? I'm worried about her.

DON *(Even more surprised)*: You're worried about *Jill*?

MRS. BAKER: Aren't you?

DON: Something's come over you. First you like my song, now you're worried about Jill. *(He thinks for a moment, then turns to her)* And you haven't mentioned my coming home for hours. Are you all right?

MRS. BAKER: Don't I seem all right?

DON: No. You're not behaving like Supermom. Next thing you'll be telling me you like Jill.

MRS. BAKER: I don't dislike her. I just wish she were a different sort of girl.

DON: She *is* a different sort of girl. That's what you don't like.

MRS. BAKER: When I was her age, punctuality meant something.

DON: What did it mean?

MRS. BAKER: It meant that if I were going to be three hours late for dinner, I'd call and explain.

DON: You would never be three hours late.

MRS. BAKER: No, I certainly would not!

DON: You'd be a month early.

MRS. BAKER: You know, she might be lost. She said she always loses her way around New York.

DON: Any cab driver could bring her home. *(With a quizzical look)* She never said she loses her way around New York.

MRS. BAKER: Oh, yes—she said it to me.

DON: If she'd said it to you, I'd've heard it.

MRS. BAKER *(Flustered)*: Well . . . I guess it was after you went out.

DON: She was in here while I was out?

MRS. BAKER: It seems to me she was . . . yes.

DON: Why?

MRS. BAKER: Oh, the usual—she wanted her dress zipped up.

DON: You did that while I was here.

MRS. BAKER: She just stopped in, that's all. She was only here a minute.

DON: What did you talk about?

MRS. BAKER: I don't remember.

DON: You remember she loses her way around New York. What else did you talk about?

MRS. BAKER: What does it matter?

DON *(Raising his voice)*: If it doesn't matter, then tell me!

MRS. BAKER: Donny, please don't shout at me! *(After a moment)* We talked about Snow White.

DON: Snow White and the Seven Dwarfs? *That* Snow White?

MRS. BAKER: Is there any other?

DON: Why were you talking about her?

MRS. BAKER *(Irritated)*: What difference does it make why we were talking about Snow White? We didn't say anything bad about her.

DON: I don't like you talking to my friends behind my back.

MRS. BAKER: It wasn't behind your back! You weren't even in the room! *(She is thoughtful for a moment as she slips off her earrings)* Donny? Did Linda Fletcher give you confidence?

DON: Mother, you know damn well what Linda Fletcher gave me, so don't be funny.

MRS. BAKER: I wasn't being funny. Did she *also* give you confidence?

DON: Yes.

MRS. BAKER: Didn't *I*?

DON: You gave me help.

MRS. BAKER: I always thought one led to the other.

DON: Not necessarily, I guess.

MRS. BAKER: Why didn't you tell me you don't like being called Donny?

DON: I told you a thousand times.

MRS. BAKER: I'd remember something I heard a thousand times.

DON: Maybe it was only a hundred. What's this all about? Why all these questions?

MRS. BAKER: What's wrong with "Donny"?

DON: It reminds me of Little Donny Dark.

MRS. BAKER: And what's wrong with that?

DON: You work on it.

MRS. BAKER: Well, what would you like to be called? I'll try to remember.

DON: Don . . . Donald. You can call me Sebastian or Irving. I don't care. Anything but Donny.

MRS. BAKER: I'm not going to call you Sebastian or Irving. I'll try to remember to call you—

> *(She is interrupted by a faint noise from JILL's apartment. They both turn toward JILL's door. The noise grows louder; it is laughter and conversation, none of it intelligible. We hear JILL's voice and a man's)*

DON *(Smiling)*: She's home! She'll be in in a minute. You can go now, Mom.

> *(MRS. BAKER goes near JILL's door and listens)*

MRS. BAKER: There's a man with her.

DON: Stop listening at the door.

MRS. BAKER: I can't hear anything. They're at the other end, but there's a man with her.

DON: That's probably the television you hear.

MRS. BAKER: Why should she be laughing and talking with a television set?

DON: Mom, please come away from there.

> *(MRS. BAKER moves away from JILL's door, noticing that DON is anxious)*

MRS. BAKER: I am away from there.

> *(There is a loud, whimsical knock at JILL's door)*

DON: Come on in!

(JILL enters, gaily, followed by RALPH AUSTIN, a young man, sloppily dressed)

JILL: Oh, hi! I'm back! I've brought Ralph Austin with me. *(Seeing MRS. BAKER)* Oh, Mrs. Baker—you're still here. *(Making introductions)* Don, this is Ralph Austin. I told you about him. He's directing the play. Ralph, this is Don, and Don's mother, Mrs. Baker. *(They exchange how-do-you-do's)* I told Ralph all about you and he was anxious to meet you.

RALPH *(In an unnaturally loud voice)*: Hey, Jill told me how with-it, how . . . how adept you are for someone who's . . . well, for someone who can't see.

DON: You can say "blind," Ralph. It's in my vocabulary, too.

RALPH: Oh, yes. *(Shouting)* I should have known that. Jill told me you have no hang-ups about the thing.

DON: Ralph, you don't have to shout.

MRS. BAKER: Mr. Austin, my son is not deaf!

RALPH *(In a normal tone)*: Oh. I'm sorry.

DON: It happens all the time. People think if you can't see, you can't hear.

JILL: He can hear a lot better than we can.

DON: No, I can't.

JILL: And what sense of smell!

> *(She looks at MRS. BAKER)*

MRS. BAKER: Can I fix you something before I go?

RALPH: We've had dinner, but I wouldn't mind some coffee if it isn't too much trouble.

MRS. BAKER: You were expected here for dinner, Jill.

> *(JILL looks over at the dining table and crosses to it, unhappily)*

JILL: Oh, Don . . . I'm sorry.

DON: It's all right.

JILL: Our flowers and candles. It's so beautiful. *(She turns back, concealing her upset with flippancy)* Well, there you are. That's me for you. I just completely forgot. We went to Ralph's place after the audition to celebrate and we drank a whole bottle of champagne or whatever it was.

RALPH: It was sparkling burgundy.

DON *(Excitedly)*: Then you got the part?

JILL: Yes and no. I'm not playing the wife.

DON: What are you playing, the homosexual?

JILL: No, his secretary. It's a small part, but I've got one good scene.

RALPH: Jill did a really great audition. Man, I was really proud of her.

JILL: God, was I nervous. It wasn't the reading, but imagine having to stand out there completely and totally naked.

(MRS. BAKER *drops a cup, which breaks)*

MRS. BAKER: Sorry, I broke a cup.

JILL: Can I help you?

MRS. BAKER *(Picking up the pieces)*: No, thank you. It's already broken. How many coffees?

DON: None for me.

JILL: I don't want any.

DON: Why did Jill have to be naked for the audition?

RALPH: Because there's a lot of nudity involved in this play. We had to see the actors' bodies. The *visual* here is very important. I hope you don't mind my saying that.

DON: Not at all.

MRS. BAKER: How do you take your coffee, Mr. Austin?

RALPH: Just black, please.

JILL: Now I don't think anyone can call me a prude.

MRS. BAKER: I'd like to see them try.

JILL: At first I hated the idea of getting completely undressed, but there were like forty or fifty actors all around me, all naked. I was the only one with clothes on. *(Turning to* MRS. BAKER*)* How would you feel?

MRS. BAKER *(Handing* RALPH *his coffee)*: Warm—all over!

RALPH: I was out front with the writer and the producer, and the minute we saw Jill naked we knew she wasn't right for the lead.

MRS. BAKER: Tell me, Mr. Austin, is there any story to this play or is that too much to hope for?

RALPH: It has a very dramatic story, Mrs. Baker.

JILL: I die at the end.

MRS. BAKER: Pneumonia?

RALPH: It's going to be a wild scene. I'm a genius at this kind of thing. Jill will be lying there on the stage dying of an overdose of heroin. She's in agony, writhing across the stage on her back—screaming this one word. She screams it over and over and over and over.

DON: What's the word?

MRS. BAKER: Did you have to ask?

RALPH: Well, uh . . . I don't know if I should use it here.

MRS. BAKER: You're going to use it on the stage, but you don't know if you should use it *here*?

DON: That's all right, you can say it. What's the word? *(RALPH crosses and whis-*

pers into DON's *ear.* DON *squirms slightly)* Maybe you'd better not.
(MRS. BAKER *sighs with relief)*

DON: Ralph, do you think the public is ready for this kind of thing?

RALPH: Are you kidding? They're dying for it. I'm talking about the *thinking* public—not those giddy little tight-assed matrons from Scarsdale *(Everyone freezes.* RALPH *slowly becomes aware of the chill in the room)* Have I said something wrong?

MRS. BAKER: Pick anything, Mr. Austin.

JILL: Ralph, Mrs. Baker lives in Scarsdale.

RALPH: Oh. *(Trying, with a big smile)* Well, present company excepted, isn't that the rule?

MRS. BAKER: I don't wish to be excepted, thank you. Tell me, what's the name of your play?

RALPH: It's called *Do Unto Others.*

MRS. BAKER: I must remember that; I'd hate to wander in by accident.

JILL: You might like it if you gave it a chance, Mrs. Baker. I mean see it with an open mind.

DON: I should warn you my mother hasn't liked anything since *The Sound of Music.*

JILL: The play isn't really dirty. I wouldn't be in a dirty play. It's true to life.

DON: Not Mom's life.

JILL: This play is really good. It just needs polishing.

MRS. BAKER: I'd've said scrubbing.

RALPH *(He sits next to* JILL, *intimately)*: We'll just have to try to make it without the support of Scarsdale.

MRS. BAKER: Well, I wouldn't count on this giddy little matron. I don't intend to pay money to see nudity, obscenity and degeneracy.

RALPH: Mrs. Baker, these things are all a part of life.

MRS. BAKER: I know, Mr. Austin. So is diarrhea, but I wouldn't classify it as entertainment.

JILL: Listen, Ralph, if this play is going to be closed by the police . . .

RALPH: Don't worry. It'll run two years and I wouldn't be surprised if it made a star out of you.

JILL: Wouldn't it be groovy to see JILL TANNER up in lights?

MRS. BAKER: Jill Tanner?

JILL: Benson is my married name, but I'm using my real name—Tanner. Please remember it. I mean it would be terrible if I became a star and nobody knew it was me.

RALPH *(Rising)*: I've got to get going. Steve is coming over with some rewrites. How long will it take you to pack?

JILL *(With an anxious glance at* DON*)*: Well . . . not long, but you go ahead.

RALPH: I'll wait if you're not going to take forever. How many bags have you got?
(A *troubled look comes to* DON's *face.* MRS. BAKER *looks at* DON, *concerned for him)*

JILL: Only two, but it'll take me a while to find things.

RALPH: I can only let you have one closet.

DON: Are you going somewhere?

JILL: Didn't I tell you? I'm moving in with Ralph. I thought I mentioned it.

MRS. BAKER: No, you didn't.

JILL: Well, Ralph thought it would be a good idea to move in with him.

RALPH: It was your idea.

JILL: It doesn't matter whose idea it was. It was a good one. *(To* DON*)* I'm not really moving away, Don. I mean it's not far from here. *(To* RALPH*)* Where is it?

RALPH: Off Christopher Street.

JILL: Is that far?

RALPH: Across town.

JILL: See? Ralph has a terrific studio apartment. Something like this, with a skylight. He hasn't got a bed like yours, but it's really great. Wait till you see it. I mean, we want you to come over whenever you like. Don't we, Ralph?

RALPH: Sure. We'll consider you one of the family.

JILL *(To* RALPH*)*: I told you you'd like Don. *(To* DON*)* We'll have some groovy times over there. You're going to love Ralph. He's one of *us.* I wish you could see him. He has a good face. I mean strong and noble. Let Don feel your face. He can tell what you look like by feeling your face. It's really a kind face.

RALPH: Go ahead, Don.

MRS. BAKER: He doesn't want to, Mr. Austin.

> *(*JILL *takes* DON's *hand and places it on* RALPH's *face.* DON *runs his fingers over* RALPH's *face. He pulls his hand away, quickly)*

RALPH: Well, it's been great meeting you, Don. See you soon, I hope. Don't take long, hon. Oh, nice to have met you, Mrs. Baker. I apologize if I offended you.

MRS. BAKER: That's quite all right, Mr. Austin. I assure you it won't happen again.

RALPH *(To* JILL, *with a parting gesture)*: Hon.

> *(*RALPH *exits through the front door, leaving* JILL, DON *and* MRS. BAKER *all looking away from each other in embarrassed silence)*

JILL: Well, I'd better start packing. I'll stop in and say good-bye before I leave.

> *(*JILL *exits to her apartment, hurriedly, closing the door behind her.* MRS. BAKER *looks at* DON, *almost unable to bear the hurt on his face)*

DON: Mom? *(*MRS. BAKER *doesn't answer; she stares at* DON, *thoughtfully)* Mom, are you here?

MRS. BAKER: Yes.

DON: I have something to tell you. You'd better sit down.

MRS. BAKER: Is it something awful?

DON: No, you'll like it, but you'd better sit down.

MRS. BAKER *(Remains standing)*: I'm sitting.

DON: I want to go home. Will you get the car, and I'll pack. Did you hear me?

MRS. BAKER: Yes.

DON: Why don't you say something?

MRS. BAKER: I intend to. I'm collecting my thoughts.

DON: Can't you do that while you get the car? I won't take long.

> *(He starts toward the bathroom)*

MRS. BAKER: Just a minute. *(*DON *turns back)* I think we ought to talk about it.

DON: *Talk* about it? I thought you'd be dancing with joy about it. Isn't that what you wanted? Isn't that why you came here today—to take me home?

MRS. BAKER: Yes.

DON: Then what is there to talk about? God, we've been talking about it all day. You said this place isn't Buckingham Palace. You said I was living in a rat hole.

MRS. BAKER: And you said it's the Taj Mahal. You said this is your home now. Why aren't *you* dancing with joy?

DON: Are you saying you don't want me to come home?

MRS. BAKER: No. I'm only saying we should talk about it. Don't misunderstand me. I still think this place is dreadful and I doubt if I'll ever like it, but I didn't choose to live here. You did. You couldn't wait to have a place of your own. You rushed into this and now you want to rush out. I think we should talk about it.

DON: Isn't it funny that we think exactly alike, but never at the same time. I . . . I can't make it now, Mom. I'm not going to make it.

MRS. BAKER: Why? Because a girl has walked out on you?

DON: Two girls. Let's don't forget Linda.

MRS. BAKER: And it may be ten girls. Girls walk out on sighted men, too, you know.

DON: Is that supposed to make me feel better?

MRS. BAKER: It's supposed to make you stop feeling sorry for yourself. You've never felt sorry for yourself before. Please don't start now. You're going to meet a lot of girls. One day you'll meet one who is capable of a permanent relationship. Jill isn't. She knows this herself. I think you're better off staying here. I don't want you coming home discouraged and defeated. You've got your music.

DON: Christ, once and for all get it into your head—I am not Little Donny Dark! I *am* discouraged! I *am* defeated! It's over!

MRS. BAKER: Do you remember the first Donny Dark story?

DON: No.

MRS. BAKER: You were five years old. We were spending the summer on Lake Winnipesaukee. Dad took you into the lake. It was the first time you'd been in any water deeper than a bathtub. You were terrified. They could hear you screaming all over New Hampshire. Dad brought you in and I put you to bed. You trembled for hours. That night I told you a story about a little blind boy who could swim the seven seas and could talk to the dolphins—

DON (Remembering, bitterly): Yeah, and the dolphins told him about enemy submarines on their way to destroy the United States Navy, and Donny Dark swam home in time to save them. What a lot of crap.

MRS. BAKER: The next day you learned to swim! I didn't write those stories hoping for a Pulitzer Prize in literature. I wrote them because I found a way to help you. Whenever you felt discouraged or defeated, I told you a Donny Dark story, and then you tried a little harder and you did a little better. Shall I make one up now—or are you man enough to handle this situation yourself?

DON: A month ago *you* didn't think I was man enough. You said I wasn't ready to leave home. Why have you changed?

MRS. BAKER: I don't know that *I've* changed. *You're* not the boy who left home a month ago. I came down here today hoping you *were*. It's hard to adjust to not being needed any more. But I can do it now. So you get on with your own life. *(Looking around the room for a moment)* I'd like to see you have some decent furniture. You need some dishes and some glasses. I don't use all those at home. I'll send some down to you.

DON: Okay.

MRS. BAKER: And I'll send some linens. You could use better ashtrays. If you fix this place up, it might not be so bad. *(Hesitantly)* Can I help you fix it up a little?

DON: Sure.

MRS. BAKER: I'll call you in the morning and we'll talk about it.

DON: Mom. I'm glad you came.

MRS. BAKER *(Looks at him for a moment, then kisses him, gently, on the cheek)*: I love you, Don.

DON: I know, Mom. I know you do. (MRS. BAKER *leaves.* DON *crosses to* JILL's *door and listens for a moment. He pulls himself out of his despair and raps at the door, gaily)* Hey! How you doin'?

(JILL *opens the door and enters carrying two suitcases)*

JILL *(Setting the bags down)*: I think I made it. Listen, I left those new dishtowels there, and the light bulbs, if you want them.

DON: I don't need them.

JILL: Well, I'll donate them to the apartment. Oh, and here's the key. *(She takes a key from her pocket, crosses to the coffee table and puts it down)* I'll leave it here on the table. Will you give it to the super? I guess you'd better have him lock this door again.

DON: I'll wait and see who moves in. It might be someone groovy.

JILL: Oh. Yeah. I hope so. Well, let's don't have a big good-bye or anything. I'll be in touch with you.

DON: Can't you stay a minute?

JILL: Well . . . once I'm going somewhere, I like to get going. You know what I mean?

DON: I'm the same way. I was just going to have a corned beef sandwich on rye. Want one?

JILL: Once I'm going somewhere, I like to get going—unless someone offers me a corned beef sandwich on rye.

DON: How 'bout a beer?

JILL: Sure. *(She crosses to the dining table)* The candles are still lit.

DON *(As he is fixing the beer and sandwich)*: I know. I'm very religious.

JILL: Where's Mama?

DON: She went home.

JILL: I didn't hear her leave. What was the verdict?

(JILL *sits on the table, resting her feet on a chair. She takes a cigarette from her bag and lights it)*

DON: She accepted my declaration of independence.

JILL: You're kidding!

DON: I must say she put up a great battle.

JILL: Maybe she should've won. I mean . . . maybe you would be better off at home.

DON: That's a switch!

JILL: I've been thinking about it.

DON: Come on, girl. It took me a whole day and three pints of blood to convince my mother. I don't want to start on you.

JILL: I like to have things done for me.

DON: Then give up Ralph and the play and move in with my mother. I'm out of mustard.

(DON *comes out of the kitchen, slightly disoriented, and almost collides with a stool)*

JILL: I don't care. What do you think of Ralph?

DON *(Looking up, surprised)*: Where are you?

JILL: I'm on the sofa.

DON: Oh. I couldn't figure where your voice was coming from.

JILL: You always could before.

DON: I . . . I wasn't concentrating. *(Handing her the plate)* He seemed very nice.

JILL: Who?

DON: Ralph.

JILL: You didn't like him, did you?

DON: I said he seemed very nice.

JILL: I could tell you didn't like him. You were a little uptight when he was here.

DON: I'm always a little uptight when there's more than one person in the room. I have to figure out who's speaking and if he's speaking to me.

JILL: I guess you didn't like him because he was rude.

DON *(Sitting on an arm of the sofa)*: Was he rude?

JILL: Well, you know, putting down Scarsdale like that to your mother.

DON: That was an accident. He didn't know she was from Scarsdale. I'm sorry you think he's rude.

JILL: I don't think he's rude.

DON: Well you said it. I didn't. *(Looking around)* Or is there someone else here?

JILL: I know he comes off as a little conceited.

DON: Tell me, Jill, do *you* like Ralph?

JILL *(With a self-conscious laugh)*: What kind of a question is that? I'm moving in with him, aren't I? Why would I move in with a guy I didn't like?

DON: That was my next question.

JILL: I'd better be going . . .

DON *(Rising quickly)*: Come to think of it, I guess I don't like Ralph.

JILL: I knew it all along. But why?

DON: Like you said—he's rude and conceited.

JILL: But I've been trying to tell you he's not like that. I knew that's what you thought, but he's not at all conceited.

DON: And thanks a lot for making me feel his face.

JILL: I thought you might like him better if you knew what he looked like. He's got a good face.

DON: To look at, maybe, but it doesn't come across to the touch.

JILL: I'm sorry about that. I hoped we could all be friends. Well, I'd better—

DON *(Quickly)*: You know something? I'm going to tell you something. *You* don't like Ralph.

JILL: Oh, God! I just packed two suitcases which are sitting right over there so I can move in with him!

DON: I don't care if you have thirteen trunks! You don't like him.

JILL: Boy, you really are too much! You think just because you're blind you can see everything!

DON: That's right—that sixth sense we've got tells me you don't like Ralph Austin! How about that? Spooky, isn't it?

JILL: No, it's just stupid. I packed two suitcases which are sitting right over there—

DON: Tell me, with Ralph is it like the Fourth of July and like Christmas?

JILL: Not exactly, but he has a kind of strength. With him it's more like . . . Labour Day.

DON: Do you think *he's* a beautiful person, too?

JILL: In many ways, yes.

DON: Has he got charisma?

JILL: Definitely!

DON: Then I'm selling mine.

JILL: You'd better hurry. It's been known to fade away.

DON: Do you love him?

JILL: Why should I answer that? No matter what I say, you've already made up your own mind about it.

DON: Go ahead, answer it! Do you love him?

JILL: Yes! In my way.

DON: This morning you told me you could never love anyone.

JILL: That was this morning. Am I allowed to change my mind or has my first statement already been passed into law by Congress?

DON: Look, I'm not the worldiest human being on the block, but I know that when you're rushing into the arms of the man you love, you don't stop for a corned beef sandwich on rye.

JILL: Which shows how little you know me. Some people wear their hearts on their sleeves—I wear my appetite.

DON: Was it something my mother said?

JILL: Was *what* something your mother said?

DON: The reason you're leaving. The reason you didn't show up for dinner. I know you didn't forget. Was it something my mother said?

JILL: *You* don't even listen to your mother. Why should I?

DON: Then why are you leaving? And don't give me that crap about loving Ralph.

JILL: I'm leaving because I want to leave. I'm free and I go when I want to go.

DON: I thought it might have something to do with me.

JILL: It has nothing whatsoever to do with you.

DON: Okay. (JILL *lights a cigarette, plops down on the sofa and looks at* DON, *disturbed)* You're scared to death of becoming involved, aren't you?

JILL: I don't want to get involved. I told you that.

DON: That's right, you told me. No responsibility, no commitments.

JILL: I have to be able to get out if I get tired of the—

DON: Tired of me?

JILL: Or anybody.

DON: What if I got tired of you?

JILL *(This hadn't occurred to her)*: Of me?

DON: Doesn't anyone ever get tired of you?

JILL: I don't hang around long enough to find out.

DON: With Ralph, you could get out any time you feel like it, but it might be harder to walk out on a blind guy, right?

JILL: The blindness has nothing to do with it. Nothing!

DON: You know goddamn well it has! You wouldn't feel a thing walking out on Ralph or Sebastian or Irving, but if you walked out on Little Donny Dark, you might hate yourself and you wouldn't like that, would you? Hate *me*—or love *me*—but don't leave because I'm blind, and don't stay because I'm blind!

JILL: Who are Sebastian and Irving?

DON: Nobody. I just made them up.

JILL: Sometimes I don't understand you. We don't think alike and I know I'd only hurt you sooner or later. I don't want to hurt you.

DON: Why not? You do it to others. Why do I rate special treatment?

JILL: I don't want to be another Linda Fletcher. She hurt you, didn't she?

DON: She helped me, too. She was there when I needed her.

JILL: I can't promise that. I don't even know where I'll be when you need me.

DON: You need me a helluva lot more than I need you!

JILL: I don't need anybody. I never did and I never will. I have to go now.

DON: I'm glad you said *have* to and not *want* to.

JILL: Boy, I finally said something right. I'll be seeing you.

DON: Yeah, I'll be seeing you. I'll think about you for years and wonder if you ever made a commitment, if you ever got involved.

JILL: I hope not.

DON: Don't worry. It won't happen—because you're emotionally retarded. Did you know that? That's why you couldn't face marriage. It's why you can't face anything permanent, anything real. You're leaving now because you're afraid you might fall in love with me, and you're too adolescent for that responsibility. And you're going to stay that way. Oh, God, I feel sorry for you—because you're crippled. I'd rather be blind.

> (JILL *leaves, closing the door behind her.* DON *stands motionless for a few seconds, then dazedly takes a few steps backward. He brushes against the arm of the sofa, which jolts him a bit. Orienting himself, he turns, goes to the dining table, and starts to clear it. Some silverware clatters to the floor; he makes a move to pick it up, but doesn't bother to complete the gesture. Instead he carries some dishes to the kitchen sink. Suddenly an idea strikes him and he makes his way across the room to the tape recorder, fumblingly turns it on. His voice is heard singing: "And you made me understand /Right from the start /I could hold your gentle hand /But never hold your heart /So why the crying? /Were our brave words lying /When we both agreed there'd be no tears in our good-bye-ing?" As if to escape the painful memory, he begins to wander around the room. When he comes up against the table he feels for the heat of the candles and bends down to blow them out; as he does so his face accidentally brushes against the flowers, and he buries his face in them for a moment. But then he rips the flowers out of the basket, and with one sweep knocks everything on the table to the floor. The gesture causes him to bump into a stool, which he hurls across the room. Staggering aimlessly, he stumbles over the sofa, and falls headlong onto the floor. One arm is pinned under him. He lies there with tears welling in his eyes, and no interest in getting up. Finally he gropes for the coffee table to raise himself, but gives up and sinks back down, weeping. The front door opens.* JILL *enters, carrying her bags. She looks around the room for* DON. *When she sees what has happened, she suppresses a scream, and sets down her bags abruptly.* DON *hears this; startled and aware of his helpless position he whirls around on the floor. Anxiously)* Who is it? . . . Who's there?

JILL *(There is a silence, then she breaks the tension)*: The news is good. It's not your mother.

DON *(Realizing it's* JILL, *and attempting to compose himself)*: What are you doing here?

> *(She crosses to him, sits beside him on the floor, and takes his hand)*

JILL *(Kissing his hand)*:What are you doing on the floor?

DON: Oh . . . I was about to have a picnic.

JILL *(Brightly)*: What a great idea—

> *(He turns to her, and she begins to laugh. Hesitant at first,* DON *joins in the laughter. He reaches out for her and they hug each other joyfully)*
> *Curtain*

AFTER THE PLAY:
QUESTIONS TO HELP UNDERSTANDING AND APPRECIATION

Theme

The theme of any play is not the story line. It is the underlying idea on which the play is based. One simple way of discovering the theme is to ask yourself, "What did it all go to show me?" or "What was it that the author was trying to get across?"
1. What do you think was the theme of *Butterflies Are Free?* What generally in the play helped you to decide your interpretation of the theme?
2. Why do you think this theme became an appropriate one for a comedy?
3. The characters in the play often provide specific clues to the theme via segments of their dialogue. Recall or find segments of the dialogue of Don Baker, Mrs. Baker, and Jill Tanner that gave you clues to the general theme of the play.
4. Why do you think the author of this play used a blind boy as a character for the theme of *Butterflies Are Free?*
5. What do you think is the connection between the title of the play and your interpretation of the theme?

Characterization

Before an actor or director starts rehearsals, he or she tries to find out exactly what kinds of people the characters in the play are. Using the four characters in *Butterflies Are Free*, create your own character inventory for each one by jotting down, in point form, what is revealed about the character by:
   —what s/he says,
   —what s/he does,
   —what s/he thinks (as far as you can imagine),
   —what others say about him or her,
   —how s/he reacts to others.
Here are some additional questions designed to increase your understanding of the four characters in this play:
1. How does each of these characters see herself/himself? (self image)
2. How do the other characters in the play see each of these characters? (mirror image)
3. What do you think was the *real* character lying behind the self image and the mirror image of Don Baker, Mrs. Baker, Jill Tanner, and Ralph Austin?
To appreciate the importance of these three "faces" of each individual,

try the following character game in class. Using a volunteer from the class, write down on a slip of paper how *you* see this person, in a few general terms. Then write down how *you think* this person sees himself. Compare what the individuals in the class have written down with what the volunteer has written down in response to the question, "How do you see yourself?" If the volunteer is willing, ask him or her to comment on those things agreed or disagreed with in the mirror image and self image notes.

4. Explain, using examples, to what extent each of the four characters was:
   a) flat? (stayed the same from the beginning of the play to the end and had only one or two characteristics)
   b) dynamic? (changed from the beginning of the play to the end and had several interesting characteristics)
   c) stereotyped? (taken from a stock list of character "types" that have been used over and over again)
   d) believable? or phony?
   e) symbolic? (e.g., Romeo and Juliet symbolize young, impetuous lovers)
5. What do you imagine each character's life being like prior to the time that he or she was first introduced in the play?

Setting

The setting of any play must always help the audience to understand the theme. It also helps the audience to interpret the play and the characters who live in that setting.

1. As soon as the curtain opens on this play, the audience glances over the scene and makes up its mind about what the setting "says." What do you think the audience decided the setting of *Butterflies Are Free* said when they first saw it?
2. In what ways was the setting appropriate to the characters who worked inside it? In what ways was it inappropriate (deliberately) to other characters?

Conflict

Without any conflict at all there is no drama. The more conflict in a play, the more "theatrically effective" it usually is. That is, the audience feels gripped, excited, involved. Interpret the basic conflicts that follow by translating them into characters in this play who are in conflict with someone or something:

— one individual against another individual,
— an individual against him/herself (usually against an inability to do something),
— an individual against a group or a segment of the population,

—an individual against the whole world,
—an individual against fate or nature.
1. To what extent did each one of these characters have his or her conflict solved?
2. What would you have done in similar conflict situations?

SHARING THE RESPONSE AFTER THE PLAY

Almost everyone likes to talk about a play or motion picture they have seen. One of the best ways to give everyone in the class a chance to respond to *Butterflies Are Free* is to break into groups for a Critics' Corner project. Use someone in each group to record what that group thought they liked or disliked about the play and why. The leader of each group then presents to the class the comments of the "critics" using the recorder's notes. Open discussion from the whole class can then provide agreement or disagreement with the comments of the critics.

The following questions might help the Critics' Corner groups to get started. In each case, answer the question in detail and provide reasons for anwers to questions 1, 3, and 4.
1. To what age and kind of people do you think this play would mostly appeal?
2. What did you, personally, enjoy most about this play?
3. Which characters did you think were most realistic? least realistic?
4. Which parts of the play did you feel were the most dramatically effective?
5. If comedy is a mirror of life with a happy ending, what aspects of *Butterflies Are Free* do you think were being used as mirrors of everyday life today?

Suspense

Suspense is that element in a play that makes the audience want to find out what happens next. It is a device guaranteed to rivet the attention of the audience on the play itself.

Describe any five instances of effective suspense in this play.

Foreshadowing

In order to involve each member of the audience with the play, the dramatist uses the technique of *foreshadowing*. This is a way of dropping clues, through the setting, dialogue, or action, in order to suggest to the audience what may happen next.

What evidence of *foreshadowing* did you find in this play?

Irony

An author uses *irony* to create a certain mental interest or excitement on the part of the audience. Decide which of the following three basic kinds of irony were present in the play:

a) Verbal irony: what is said is the opposite to what was really meant (e.g., "Welcome to Buckingham Palace," said the young bachelor as he opened the door to his pad.)

b) Situation irony: the situation is in contrast to what is expected (e.g., The happy, cheering crowd made its way up the gangplank of this great ocean liner on its maiden voyage and threw garlands over the gleaming nameplate. The name of the ship was *The Titanic*.)

c) Dramatic irony: the audience knows something that the character on the stage does not (e.g., "You'll never taste wine as good as this again," said the old ladies on stage as they offered their poisoned elderberry wine to the unsuspecting visitor.)

Introduction to
A THOUSAND CLOWNS

The critics agreed with the freshness and the sharp humour of *A Thousand Clowns:*

"A pleasant surprise."

"Bright and joyfully mocking."

"Humour springs naturally out of honest characterization and real conflict."

The play deals optimistically with one basic idea: we all have unique, fascinating personalities waiting to break out and discover the world and waiting to be discovered by others, if only society would stop stifling our individualism. Anyone who has ever felt that life was becoming a rat race or that it was becoming impossible to be oneself would probably find that *A Thousand Clowns* strikes a familiar chord.

The author, Herb Gardner, wrote *A Thousand Clowns* as his first full-length play at the age of twenty-eight. He had previously sold cartoons that seemed to be based on the idea that most people are funny, if the observer has a sense of humour.

Gardner's comedy seemed to be in tune with the times. The confused Sixties was a time when many young people were in revolt against the establishment. The Beatles thumbed their noses at the conventions of the older generation; Ken Kesey satirized regimentation and authority in *One Flew Over the Cuckoo's Nest.* Television situation comedies gradually became satires based on the conflicts that result from different life styles. It was in this general atmosphere of making fun of the way people live their lives that *A Thousand Clowns* was written and later filmed.

As with *Butterflies Are Free,* you might warm up for the impact of this comedy by discussing answers to some questions designed to lead you into many of the ideas included in the play.

1. Although the characters introduced in this comedy are, in general, very different from one another, they seem to be attracted to one another.

   Why do you think so many opposites often attract while likes often repel?

2. Jason Robards, who played the lead in this play, said in an interview that he loved the idea of playing the part of a man who "is the sidewalk superintendent of the human race."

Discuss what he might have meant by the phrase "sidewalk superintendent of the human race." Share some of your personal experiences of having played this role both in and out of school.

3. The hero of this play has been described as "a nonconformist who worries about getting mothered by the world."
   What do you think this unusual statement means?

4. Why do you think so many adults seem to spend their lives following set daily routines and are involved in the "rat race?"
   Suggest examples of this in daily life at school.
   How would you suggest remedying the situation?
   What kind of job or career do you have in mind that might avoid the so-called "rat race"?

5. Some people are "weekend livers" after a week of daily routine.
   What are some of the things you do on weekends that are not directed by the rules or pressures of others?

CASTING THE PLAY FOR A PLAY-READING OR WALKTHROUGH PRODUCTION

Play-reading: reading the dialogue as dramatically as possible using individual students "cast" by the class, with your teacher reading the non-dialogue sections.

Walkthrough production: similar to play-reading but with the addition of hand-held play scripts, and the use of the front of the class as an acting area. Movement, gesture, facial expression, and simple props accompany the dramatic reading of the dialogue.

Before the play-reading or the walkthrough production of *A Thousand Clowns*, it is a good idea for the whole class to suggest who would probably be able to project well each character in the play. The following brief notes on the play's characters will help you to cast the play. They are the kind of quick descriptions a casting director might have in mind when choosing actors for their roles.

MURRAY BURNS
—a former gag-writer for a kiddie TV show
—an eccentric with an off-beat sense of humour
—a sidewalk superintendent of the human race
—an energetic, liberated, free thinker, who is considered "odd" by his brother, Arnold

SANDRA MARKOWITZ
—a budding psychologist, three months out of college

—a woman who gets a laugh from the audience with each fountain of tears
—a psychologist who knows she gets too involved with her cases
—a warmhearted, sensitive worker

ALBERT AMUNDSEN
—Sandra's supervisor and leader of the case study team
—a scientist who is always in professional control
—a believer in having a detailed file on every case
—a middle-aged man—of twenty-eight years old!

NICK BURNS
—a worldly wise, twelve-year-old nephew who lives with his uncle, Murray Burns
—a self-conscious and precocious child
—a young boy who loves his uncle but fears that he will be taken away by the social welfare authorities

ARNOLD BURNS
—Murray Burns' sensible, down-to-earth, hardworking older brother
—an experienced job agent in his early forties
—a man who likes to maintain his dignity

LEO HERMAN
—an actor who plays Chuckles the Chipmunk in a TV kiddie show
—his work on Chuckles the Chipmunk is beginning to get to him
—he can go wildly insane

ALTERNATIVES: AUDIO-VISUAL PRESENTATIONS

The following alternatives to play-reading and to walkthrough production are suggested for individuals and groups who prefer to present the play via audio-visual equipment:

Using 35 mm slides and accompanying dialogue from selected scenes

A presentation of 36 slides (35 mm) of selected scenes with accompanying dialogue can be made. The dialogue could be spoken either live or recorded.
The slides could be:
a) taken candid-camera style in and out of school,
b) photographed in a room or drama studio as a series of stills from selected scenes,
c) photographed magazine illustrations or segments of advertisement

graphics that suggest similar situations to the scenes from the play, with accompanying dialogue.

Using video camera and recorder or 8 mm sound movie camera

The class divides into groups, each group presenting its own 5-minute sequence from the play. These are to be chosen from a number of sequences suggested by the whole class, in order from beginning to end. The lines will need to be learned beforehand. If the 8 mm silent camera is used, play segments could be chosen for their ability to suggest visual associations. For example, Murray Burns has some long speeches in the play that reveal his thoughts on the human race. These speeches could be recorded on audiotape. The 8 mm camera could then be used to visualize Murray's comments on the "human race."

A THOUSAND CLOWNS

Herb Gardner

In complete darkness, before the curtain goes up, we hear the voice of Chuckles the Chipmunk.

CHUCKLES' VOICE *(Intimately, softly)*: Goshes and gollygoods, kidderoonies; now what're all us Chippermunkies gonna play first this fine mornin'?
CHORUS OF KIDS: Gonna play Chuckle-Chip Dancing.
CHUCKLES' VOICE: And with who?
CHORUS OF KIDS: With you!
CHUCKLES' VOICE *(Louder)*: And who is me?
CHORUS OF KIDS *(Screaming)*: Chuckles the Chippermunkie! Rayyy-yyyyyyyyyyyy.

> The curtain goes up on this last screaming syllable, revealing MURRAY BURNS' one-room apartment. The voices of Chuckles and the kids continue but are now coming from an ancient table-model T.V. set at the left. The set is facing away from the audience and is being watched by NICHOLAS BURNS, a twelve-year-old. The apartment is on the second floor of a brownstone on the lower West Side of Manhattan. It consists of one large, high-ceilinged room in which borrowed furniture rambles in no meaningful arrangement—some gaudy, some impractical, no matching pieces. It is obvious from MURRAY BURNS' apartment that he is a collector, though it is not entirely clear just what he is a collector of. All about the room, on the floor, on the coffee table, on dresser tops, is MURRAY's collection: eighteen broken radios, some with interesting cathedral-style cabinets; over two dozen elaborately disabled clocks of different sizes, some of them on the wall; parts of eight Victrolas, mostly cabinets; a variety of hats, including a Prussian helmet and a deerstalker; a pirate pistol; a bugle; a megaphone; and stacks of magazines and books. It is somehow, though, a very comfortable-looking apartment. There is an alcove at the left, with a small bed, a child's desk and some bookshelves. This is NICK's part of the place and it is very neat, ordered, organized, seeming almost to have nothing to do with the main room. There is a bathroom door at left below the small alcove. Right of the alcove are three large windows and a built-in window seat. A closed venetian blind covers all three windows. At centre is a large, comfortable rumpled bed with an elaborate wooden headboard running up the wall almost to the ceiling. The headboard is loaded with clocks, radios, and two lamps. At right is the entrance door to the apartment. To the left of the door are two large office-style filing cabinets in which MURRAY keeps some of his clothes, and to the right is a bureau covered with knickknacks on which MURRAY's hats are hung. Downstage right is the kitchen door; to the left of it is a desk buried under papers, and built-in bookshelves stuffed with a jumble of books and nonsense. There is a closet to the left of the desk. A Morris chair and an armless swivel chair are on either side of a small table at right and there is a brightly coloured beach chair at left in front of the windows.
>
> AT RISE: *It is eight-thirty on a Monday morning; it is rather dark, the only real light is a scattered haze from the television set. The chorus of kids is now singing the "Chuckles Song." NICK watches expressionlessly.*

CHORUS OF KIDS *(Singing)*: Who's whitcha at—eight-thirty?
    Whose face is so—so dirty?
    Who's sparky—who's spunky?
    Chip, Chip, Chip, Chip—Chippermunkie!

NICK *(Quietly)*: Oh, this is terrible. This is rotten.

CHORUS OF KIDS: Who's always good—for funnin'? Whose scooter-bike—keeps runnin'?

    (MURRAY enters from the kitchen carrying a cup of coffee; he is in his mid-thirties. He is wearing shorts and an undershirt and is not quite awake yet.)

MURRAY *(Walking across to the bed)*: Get those kids outa here. *(Sits on the bed.)* Nick, what'd I tell you about bringing your friends in here this early in the morning?

NICK: It's not my friends; it's the T.V.

MURRAY: Play with your friends outside. Get those kids out of here. *(NICK turns the set off. MURRAY looks over at the front door, waves at it and shouts.)* Good. And none of you kids come back here till this afternoon.

NICK: It wasn't my friends. It was Chuckles the Chipmunk.

MURRAY *(Sleepily)*: That's very comforting.

NICK *(Brings a pack of cigarettes to MURRAY)*: Boy, it's a terrible program now. It was a much better show when you were writing it.

MURRAY: When Sandburg and Faulkner quit, I quit. What kind of a day is it outside?

NICK *(Going to the kitchen)*: It's a Monday.

MURRAY: I mean warm or cold or sunny is what I mean.

NICK: I haven't been outside yet.

MURRAY *(He pulls the blind up revealing the windows; there is no change whatever in the lighting, the room remains dark. The windows have no view other than the gray blank wall of the building a few feet opposite)*: Ah, light. *(He leans out of the window, cranes his head around to look up at the sky.)* Can't see a thing. Not a thing. *(Pulls his head back in.)* No matter what time of day or what season, we got a permanent fixture out there; twilight in February.

NICK *(Bringing the coffee pot out of the kitchen and filling MURRAY's cup)*: You better call the weather record like always.

MURRAY: One morning I'll wake up and that damn building'll have fallen down into Seventh Avenue so I can see the weather. *(Picks up the phone; dialing.)* Using a machine to call up another machine. I do not enjoy the company of ghosts. *(Into the phone)* Hello, Weather Lady! Well, I'm just fine, and how is your nasal little self this morning? What's the weather? Uh-huh. That high? And the wind, which way does the wind blow this morning? Ah, good. Uh-huh, all the way to East Point and Block Island. Humidity? Very decent. Whoops, oh, there you go again. You simply *must* learn not to repeat yourself. I keep telling you every morning that once is enough. You'll never learn. *(Hangs up.)* Women seldom sense when they have become boring. *(Goes to the window again, leans out, raises his voice, shouting out of the window.)* Neighbours, I have an announcement for you. I have *never seen* such a collection of dirty windows. Now I want to see you all out there on the fire escape with your Mr. Clean bottles, and let's snap it up . . .

NICK: Gee, Murray, you gotta shout like that every morning?

MURRAY: It clears my head. *(After glancing around clock-filled apartment)* What time is it?

NICK: It's eight-forty.

MURRAY: Well, what're you doing here? Why aren't you in school?

NICK: It's a holiday. It's Irving R. Feldman's birthday, like you said.

MURRAY: Irving R. Feldman's birthday is my own personal national holiday. I did not open it up for the public. He is proprietor of perhaps the most distinguished kosher delicatessen in this neighbourhood and as such I hold the day of his birth in reverence.

NICK: You said you weren't going to look for work today because it was Irving R. Feldman's birthday, so I figured I would celebrate too, a little.

MURRAY: Don't kid *me*, Nick, you know you're supposed to be in school. I thought you *liked* that damn genius' school—why the hell—

NICK: Well, I figured I'd better stay home today till you got up. *(Hesitantly)* There's something I gotta discuss with you. See, because it's this special school for big brains they watch you and take notes and make reports and smile at you a lot. And there's this psychologist who talks to you every week, each kid separately. He's the biggest smiler they got up there.

MURRAY: Because you got brains they figure you're nuts.

NICK: Anyway, we had Show and Tell time in Mrs. Zimmerman's class on Monday, and each kid in the class is supposed to tell about some trip he took and show pictures. Well, y'remember when I made you take me with you to the El Bambino Club over on Fifty-second?

MURRAY: Nick . . . you showed and you told.

NICK: Well, it turned out they're very square up at the Revere School. And sometimes in class, when we have our Wednesday Free-Association-Talk Period, I sometimes quote you on different opinions . . .

MURRAY: That wasn't a good idea.

NICK: Well, I didn't know they were such nervous people there. Murray, they're very nervous there. And then there was this composition I wrote in Creative Writing about the advantages of Unemployment Insurance.

MURRAY: Why did you write about that?

NICK: It was just on my mind. Then once they got my record out they started to notice what they call "significant data." Turns out they've been keeping this file on me for a long time, and checking with that Child Welfare place; same place you got those letters from.

MURRAY: I never answer letters from large organizations.

NICK: So, Murray . . . when they come over here, I figure we'd better . . .

MURRAY: When they come over here?

NICK: Yeah, this Child Welfare crowd, they want to take a look at our environment here.

MURRAY: Oh, that's charming. Why didn't you tell me about this before, Nick?

NICK: Well, y'know, the past coupla nights we couldn't get together.

MURRAY: That was unavoidable. You know when I have a lot of work you stay up at Mrs. Myers'.

NICK: *(Pointing at the dresser)*: Murray; your work forgot her gloves last night.

MURRAY: That's very bright.

NICK: Anyway, for this Child Welfare crowd, I figure we better set up some kind of story before they get here.

MURRAY: You make it sound like a vice raid.

NICK: I mean, for one thing, you don't even have a job right now.

MURRAY: Look, you want me to put up some kind of front when they get here? O.K., I will. Don't worry, kid. I'll snow 'em good.

NICK: I thought maybe you could at least look in the papers for a job, this morning before they get here. So we could tell them about your possibilities.

MURRAY *(Without much conviction)*: I look every day.

NICK: Couldn't I just read you from the *Times* again like last week? While you get dressed?

MURRAY: O.K., read me from the paper. *(He starts to get dressed.)*

NICK: And then, maybe, you'll take a shave?

MURRAY: All right, all right.

NICK *(Picking up the* Times *from the swivel chair)*: This paper is three days old.

MURRAY: So what do you want me to do, bury it? Is it starting to rot or something? Read me from the paper.

NICK: But most of these jobs, somebody must have taken them. Look, I'll go down and get a newer—

MURRAY: We do *not* need a newer paper. All the really important jobs stay forever. Now start on the first page of Help-Wanted-Male and read me from the paper.

NICK: O.K. *(Puts on his glasses; reads aloud.)* "Administ, Exoppty. To ninety dollars." What's that?

MURRAY: Administrative Assistant, excellent opportunity. Nothing. Keep reading.

NICK: But ninety dollars would be ninety dollars more than nothing. Nothing is what you make now.

MURRAY: Have you ever considered being the first twelve-year-old boy in space?

NICK: But, ninety dollars . . .

MURRAY: *You* go be an Administ, Exoppty. They *need* men like you. Read further.

NICK *(Reading from the paper)*: "Versatile Junior, traffic manager, industrial representative organization. One hundred to one hundred twenty-five dollars. Call Mr. Shiffman."

MURRAY *(Picks up the cardboard from his shirt collar and talks into it)*: Hello, Mr. Shiffman? I read your name in the New York *Times,* so I know you must be real. My name is Mandrake the Magician. I am a versatile Junior and I would like to manage your traffic for you. You see, sir, it has long been my ambition to work in a pointless job, with no future and a cretin like you as my boss . . .

NICK: But, Murray, it says "one hundred twenty-five dollars," that's a lot of . . .

MURRAY: Just read the ads. No editorial comment or personal recommendations. When I need your advice, I'll ask for it. Out of the mouths of babes comes drooling.

NICK: You said that last week. Murray, you don't want a job is the whole thing.

MURRAY: Would you just concentrate on being a child? Because I find your imitation of an adult hopelessly inadequate.

NICK: You want to be your own boss, but the trouble with that is you don't pay yourself anything. (NICK *decides that what he has just said is very funny. He laughs.)* Hey—you don't pay yourself anything—that's a good line—I gotta remember that.

MURRAY: That's what *you* said last week.

NICK: Look, Murray. *(He puts the paper down and stands up.)* Can I speak to you man to man?

MURRAY: That was cute about a year ago, buddy, but that line has got to go.

NICK *(Takes off his glasses)*: Murray, I am upset. For me as an actual child the way you live in this house and we live is a dangerous thing for my later life when I become an actual person. An unemployed person like you are for so many months is bad for you as the person involved and is definitely bad for me who he lives with in the same house where the rent isn't paid for months sometimes. And I wish you would get a job, Murray. Please.

> (MURRAY *tries to control himself but cannot hide his laughter; he sees that* NICK *is offended by this and tries to stop.* NICK *walks away from him, goes to his alcove.*)

MURRAY *(Goes to* NICK *in the alcove)*: Kid, I know. I'm sorry. You're right. You are. This *is* terrible.

NICK: You're not kidding.

MURRAY: Nick.

NICK: Yeah?

MURRAY: Nick, y'know when I said I was looking for work last week? *(Somewhat ashamed)* Well, I went to the movies. Every day. In the afternoon.

NICK: *Murray,* you mean you really . . .

MURRAY: Now don't give me any of that indignant crap. I happen to be admitting something to you, and it is bad enough I should have to discuss my adult problems with a grotesque cherub, without you giving me dirty looks on top of it. Swell crowd in the movies on a weekday working afternoon. Nobody sits next to anybody, everybody there figures that everybody else is a creep; and *all* of them are right. *(Suddenly smiling, taking* NICK's *arm, trying to change the subject)* Have you ever been to the top of the Empire State Building?

NICK: Yes. Six times. With you. In November.

MURRAY: Oh, really? Have you ever been to the Statue of Liberty?

NICK: No.

MURRAY: Today is Irving R. Feldman's birthday. We will go to the top of the Statue of Liberty and watch the *Queen Elizabeth* come in, full of those tired, poor, huddled masses yearning to breathe free.

NICK: Murray, why did you go to the movies in the middle of the afternoon when you said you were looking for work?

MURRAY: There's a window right in her navel, we will look out and see . . .

NICK: What is it? Were you very tired, or what?

MURRAY *(Sits down in his chair)*: See, last week I was going to check with Uncle Arnie and some of the other agents about writing for some of the new T.V. shows. I was on the subway, on my way there, and I got off at Forty-second Street and went to the movies. *(He leans back in his chair, lights a cigarette;* NICK *sits opposite him on the bed.)* There are eleven movie houses on that street, Nick. It is Movieland. It breathes that seductive, carpety, minty air of the inside of movie houses. Almost as irresistible for me as pastrami. Now, there is the big question as you approach the box office, with the sun shining right down the middle of a working day, whether everybody going in is as embarrassed as you are. But once you are past the awkward stage, and have gotten your ticket torn by the old man inside, all doubts just go away. Because it is dark. And inside it is such a scene as to fracture the imagination of even a nut like yourself, Nick, because inside it is lovely and a little damp and nobody can see you, and the dialogue is falling like rain on a roof and you are sitting deep in front of a roaring, colour, Cinemascope, stereophonic, nerve-cooling, heart-warming, spine-softening, perfect-happy-ending picture show and it is Peacefulville, U.S.A. There are men there with neat mustaches who have shaved, and shined their shoes and put on a tie even, to come and sit alone in the movies. And there are near-sighted cute pink ladies who eat secret caramels; and very old men who sleep; and the *ushers;* buddy, you are not kidding *these* boys. They know you are not there because you are waiting for a train, or you are on a vacation, or you work a night job. They know you are there to *see* the *movie.* It is the business and the purpose of your day, and these boys give you their sneaky smile to show you that they know. *(Depressed by his own words; quietly, almost to himself)* Now the moral question for me here, is this: When one is faced with life in the bare-assed, job-hunting raw on the one hand, and eleven fifty-cent double features on the other, what is the mature, sensible, and mentally healthy step to take? *(He is slumped in his chair now.)*

NICK *(Seeing MURRAY's depression; softly, with concern)*: What's wrong, Murray?

MURRAY *(Walks slowly to the window, leans against the wall, looks sadly out of the window; speaks quietly)*: I don't know. I'm not sure.

NICK: Hey, Murray, you all right . . .? *(He goes to MURRAY, touches his arm. Then smiling suddenly in an attempt to cheer him)* Murray, let's go to the Statue of Liberty.

> *(MURRAY turns, laughs in agreement, and NICK starts for his jacket while MURRAY puts his binoculars around his neck and begins putting on his jacket. The doorbell rings. NICK looks at MURRAY, then goes to answer it. NICK is holding the front door only part-way open, hesitating to let in two people we now see standing outside in the hall. They are ALBERT AMUNDSON and SANDRA MARKOWITZ. ALBERT, graduate of N.Y.U.'s School of Social Work, is a middle-aged man of twenty-eight; SANDRA, though a pretty girl of twenty-five, wears clothes obviously more suited to a much older woman. ALBERT carries a small briefcase and SANDRA carries two manila file envelopes and a gigantic handbag.)*

ALBERT: Hello, young man, I am Mr. Amundson, this is Miss Markowitz. We would like to speak to your uncle.

NICK *(Still not opening the door all the way)*: Well, I don't know if . . .

ALBERT: Isn't he in?

MURRAY: Hello.

ALBERT: How do you do, Mr. Burns. Miss Markowitz and I are a Social Service unit assigned to the New York Bureau of Child Welfare. We have been asked by the Bureau to—May we come in?

MURRAY: Certainly.

> *(Nick opens the door all the way, letting them both into the main room.)*

ALBERT: We, Miss Markowitz and I, have been asked by the B.C.W. to investigate and examine certain pupils of the Revere School. There is certain information which the school and the city would like to have, regarding young Nicholas.

MURRAY: Sit down, Miss Markowitz, please. Mr. Amundson. I'll just get rid of these things.

> *(MURRAY takes pants, shirts, a bugle, a clock, a yoyo, a half-empty bag of peanuts and an ashtray off the chairs, and with one sweeping movement puts all of them on the bed. The three of them take seats around the coffee table, NICK standing nervously off to one side.)*

ALBERT: I'd like to explain just why we are here, Mr. Burns . . .

NICK: Would anybody like some coffee?

ALBERT: Why, thank you, Nicholas. Miss Markowitz?

SANDRA: Yes, thank you.

NICK *(Whispering to* MURRAY *on his way to the kitchen)*: Watch it.

ALBERT *(Smiling politely)*: It might be best, Mr. Burns, for the child if perhaps you sent him downstairs to play or something, while we have our discussion. Your case is . . .

MURRAY: Our "case." I had no idea we were a "case."

ALBERT: We do have a file on certain students at Revere.

MURRAY: So we're on file somewhere. Are we a great big, fat file, or a li'l teeny file?

ALBERT: Due to the fact that you have chosen not to answer our letters and several of our phone calls, there are many areas in which the file is incomplete, several questions—Mr. Burns, it might be better if the child went outside . . .

MURRAY: You gonna talk dirty?

ALBERT: It would be more advisable for the child not to be present, since Miss Markowitz, who will be discussing the psychological area . . . that is, we will be discussing certain matters which . . .

NICK *(From the kitchen)*: Cream and sugar for everybody?

ALBERT *(To the kitchen)*: Yes, Nicholas. *(To* MURRAY *again.)* Mr. Burns, it's going to be awkward, with the child present, to . . .

MURRAY *(To* SANDRA*)*: Miss Markowitz, may I know your first name?

SANDRA: Sandra.

MURRAY: And you are the psychologist part of this team, Sandy?

SANDRA: That's right, Mr. Burns.

MURRAY *(To* ALBERT*)*: And you, I take it, are the brawn of the outfit?

ALBERT: Perhaps I should explain, Mr. Burns, that the Social Service teams which serve Revere School are a carefully planned balance of Social Case Worker, such as myself, and Psychological Social Worker, such as Miss Markowitz, or, actually, *Dr.* Markowitz. (NICK *enters from the kitchen with four cups, gives one each to* ALBERT, SANDRA, MURRAY; *keeps one for himself.)* Mr. Burns, it is not easy to define those elements, those influences and problems which go into the make-up of a young boy.

MURRAY: I thought it was just frogs and snails and puppy dogs' tails.

ALBERT *(Using once again his polite smile)*: I appreciate the informality with which you approach this meeting, Mr. Burns, but on the more serious side, if I may, Miss Markowitz and I have a few matters . . .

NICK: Is the coffee any good?

ALBERT: Yes, very good. Thank you, Nicholas.

SANDRA: Very nice, Nicholas. *(She sees the cup in* NICK's *hand, speaks with professional interest.)* Are you drinking coffee, Nicholas? Don't you think it would be better if . . .

NICK: No. Milk. I like to drink it from a cup.

MURRAY *(To* SANDRA, *smiling)*: Now aren't you ashamed of yourself?

ALBERT *(Taking a rather large file out of his briefcase)*: Now, to plunge right in here . . .

MURRAY: Sometimes I put his milk in a shot glass. Better for getting him to drink it than adding chocolate syrup.

SANDRA *(Firmly)*: Mr. Burns, Mr. Amundson and I have several cases to examine today, and we would appreciate a certain amount of cooperation . . .

MURRAY *(To* NICK*)*: East Bronx, Mosholu Parkway.

NICK *(Looks at* SANDRA, *then to* MURRAY*)*: With a couple of years in maybe Massachusetts.

MURRAY: No Massachusetts at all. Complete Bronx.

SANDRA: I don't understand what . . .

MURRAY *(Sitting on the beach chair)*: Oh, excuse me. Nick and I are merely testing our sense of voice and accent. Nick insists he's better at it than I am.

SANDRA *(Smiling)*: As a matter of fact, the Bronx is right, but it's Grand Concourse.

MURRAY: The Massachusetts thing, way off, right?

SANDRA: Actually I took my graduate work with a professor, a man with a very strong New England accent, who could very well've influenced my speech. Nick is quite right.

NICK *(Proudly)*: Thank you, lady.

SANDRA: You certainly have a fine ear for sound, Nick. Do you and your uncle play many of these sorts of games together?

NICK: Oh, yes. We play many wholesome and constructive-type games together.

MURRAY: You're a big phony, Nick. Miss Markowitz has beautiful hazel eyes that have read many case histories and are ever watchful, and even clever little boys are not going to snow her. The lady is here for the facts.

ALBERT: Quite so, Mr. Burns. But facts alone cannot complete our examination. *(He takes out a pen, opens to a blank page in the file.)* We wish to understand . . .

NICK *(To SANDRA, showing off for her)*: Jersey City, maybe Newark. And . . . a little bit of Chicago.

MURRAY: Uh-huh. Think you've hit it, Nick.

SANDRA: That's really quite remarkable. Albert—Mr. Amundson *is* from New Jersey, and he went to Chicago University for several . . .

ALBERT *(Firmly)*: This is really quite beside the point, Sandra . . .

SANDRA: I just think it's quite remarkable, Albert, the boy's ability to . . .

ALBERT *(Purposely interrupting her)*: Suppose I just plunge right in here, before Dr. Markowitz begins her part of the interview . . .

> *(There is a noise at the front door and ARNOLD BURNS enters. He is carrying a medium-sized grocery delivery carton filled with a variety of fruit. He makes a rather incongruous delivery boy in that he is in his early forties and dressed in expensive, distinguished clothes, top coat, and hat. He is MURRAY's older brother, and his agent. It is obvious in the way he enters and automatically sets the delivery carton down on the desk that this is a daily ritual enacted at this same time every day and in this same manner. MURRAY does not even look up to greet him and NICK makes some casually mumbled greeting in his direction.)*

ARNOLD: The honeydew melon's in season again but not really ripe yet so . . . *(He turns, sees that there are strangers there.)* Oh, sorry. Didn't know you had company . . .*(Turns, goes to the door.)* See you, Nick.

NICK: Yeah, see you, Uncle Arnie. *(ARNOLD exits.)*

ALBERT *(Looking at the door)*: There is somebody else living here with you?

MURRAY: No. That's just my brother, Arnold. He brings fruit every morning on his way to the office. He's a fruit nut.

ALBERT : I see here in the file that our research team spoke to your brother; your agent, I believe. We also called the people at your last business address, N.B.C. . . .

MURRAY *(Rising)*: You really do a lot of that stuff, calling people, going into my personal . . .

ALBERT: You've refused for quite some time, Mr. Burns, to answer any of our regular inquiries. We understand that you have been unemployed at this point for nearly five months.

NICK *(To* ALBERT*)*: He has an excellent opportunity to be an administrative assistant . . .

ALBERT *(Pressing forward)*: Other than your activities as free-lance script writer, I understand that you wrote regularly for an N.B.C. program for several years.

MURRAY: I was chief writer for Leo Herman, better known as Chuckles the Chipmunk, friend of the young'uns, and seller of Chuckle-Chips, the potato chips your friend Chuckles the Chipmunk eats and chuckles over.

ALBERT: And the circumstances under which you left the employ of . . .

MURRAY: I quit.

ALBERT: You felt that this was not the work you . . .

MURRAY: I felt that I was not reaching all the boys and girls out there in Television-land. Actually it was not so much that I wasn't reaching the boys and girls, but the boys and girls were starting to reach *me*. Six months ago, a perfectly adult bartender asked me if I wanted an onion in my martini, and I said, "Gosh n' gollies, you betcha." I knew it was time to quit.

ALBERT: May I ask if this is a pattern; that is, in the past, has there been much shifting of position?

MURRAY: I *always* take an onion in my martini. This is a constant and unswerving . . .

> *(NICK, concerned with* MURRAY's *behaviour, goes toward him in an attempt to quiet him down.)*

SANDRA *(Firmly, standing)*: Mr. Burns. Perhaps you are not aware of just how serious your situation is. This entire matter is a subject of intense interest to the B.C.W. The circumstances of this child's environment, the danger of . . .

ALBERT: Our investigation, Mr. Burns, is the result of what the Bureau considers to be almost an emergency case.

NICK: He just likes to kid around, lady. But, see, we really got a great environment here . . .

MURRAY *(To* NICK*)*: Relax, kid. *(To* ALBERT *and* SANDRA*)* Look, people, I'm sorry. Let's get back to the questions.

SANDRA: Fine. Nick, suppose you and I have a little chat right here.

NICK *(As he sits down next to her)*: Fine. I was gonna suggest that myself.

SANDRA: Nick, I bet you love to come home when you've been out playing and you get tired. You say to yourself, "Gee, I'd like to go home now."

NICK: Sure, right. And I'm happy here. Boy, if you think I'm happy now, you should see me when I'm *really* happy.

MURRAY *(To* SANDRA, *sympathetically)*: He's on to you, honey. You're gonna have to be a lot foxier than that . . .

SANDRA: And I'm sure that you and your uncle have a great deal of fun together.

NICK: It's not *all* laughs.

SANDRA: Oh, I'm sure there are times when the fun stops and you have nice talks and your uncle teaches you things, helps you to . . .

NICK: I can do a great Peter Lorre imitation. Murray taught me.

ALBERT: Nicky, what Miss Markowitz means, is that you and your uncle must sometimes . . .

NICK *(In the voice of Peter Lorre, a rather good imitation)*: You can't hang me . . . I didn't do it, I tell you . . . that's not my knife . . . I am innocent . . . it's all a mistake . . .

(MURRAY *beams, smiles proudly during imitation.*)

ALBERT: Nicky, that's not what we meant, we . . .

MURRAY: What's the trouble? That happens to be a very good imitation.

ALBERT: Perhaps; but we are trying to . . .

MURRAY: Can *you* imitate Peter Lorre?

NICK *(Confidentially, to* SANDRA): I can do a pretty good James Cagney; I mean it's not fantastic like my Peter Lorre, but it . . .

ALBERT *(Raising his voice a bit, somewhat commanding)*: Nicholas, please. Try to pay attention. Now if I may proceed to . . .

SANDRA *(Aside, to* ALBERT, *somewhat annoyed with him)*: Albert, if you'll just let me handle this area. *(Then, to* NICK) Nick, let's talk about games. O.K.?

NICK: O.K.

SANDRA: Now, what kind of games do you like the best?

NICK: Mostly I like educational games and things like that. Murray gets me to develop my natural inquiring mind.

SANDRA: I wonder, do you have any favourite games or toys you'd like to show me? Some plaything that is just the most favourite one of all?

NICK: I just now threw away my collection of *National Geographics* and other educational-type magazines I had a whole collection of . . .

ALBERT: Nicky, Miss Markowitz is very interested in you and cares about you and everything. And if you brought out some of your favourite toys and playthings for her to see, I'm sure that she'd love them just as much as you do.

NICK: Well, there's Bubbles . . . *(He gets up to get it for them.)*

MURRAY: I don't think you'd be interested in seeing Bubbles . . .

(NICK *goes to a cardboard carton at the bureau, opens it, and takes out a twenty-four-inch-high plastic statue of a bare-chested hula girl. The statue is in bright colours and has an electric switch as its pedestal.* NICK *places the statue on the table between* ALBERT *and* SANDRA *and turns it on.)*

NICK: Bubbles is what you'd call an electric statue. *(The breasts of the statue light up and continue to blink on and off in spectacular fashion for the next part of the scene.* ALBERT *looks at the statue, begins busily going through the file on his lap.* SANDRA *regards the statue scientifically, professionally.* NICK *smiles proudly over his possession.)* It's got an electric battery timer in there that makes it go on and off like that.

SANDRA: Nick, is this your favourite toy?

NICK: Well, after a while it gets pretty boring. But it's a swell gimmick. There was another one in the store that was even better . . .

MURRAY: Anybody want orange juice or toast or anything?

SANDRA: Nick, tell me . . . do you like best the fact that the chest of the lady lights up?

NICK: Well, you got to admit, you don't see boobies like that every day. You want to see the effect when the lights are out? When the room is dark?

SANDRA: Tell me, Nick, is *that* what you like best about it, that you can be alone in the dark with it?

NICK: Well, I don't know. But in the dark they really knock your eyes out.

(ALBERT *is blinking nervously at the blinking lights of the statue.)*

ALBERT *(With strenuous calm)*: Perhaps, don't you think we ought to switch it off, turn off the . . .

SANDRA: Nick, does Bubbles, does she in any way, does her face remind you at all of, oh, let me see, your mother, for example?

NICK *(He looks at the face of the statue)*: No. I mean, it's just a doll, it's not a statue of anybody I know. I got it in this store downtown.

SANDRA: Her chest, is that something which . . .

NICK *(Smiling broadly)*: It's *something* all right, isn't it?

SANDRA: When you think of your mother, do you . . .

NICK: I don't think about her much.

SANDRA: But when you *do* think of her, do you remember her face best, or her *hands,* or . . .

NICK: I remember she has this terrific laugh. The kind of laugh that when she laughs it makes you laugh too. Of course, she overdoes that a lot.

SANDRA: I mean, physically, when you think of her, do you, well, when you see Bubbles, and Bubbles goes on and off like that . . .

MURRAY: Sandra, his mother's chest did not light up. Let's get that settled right now; mark it down in the file.

ALBERT *(Nervously; pointing at the blinking statue)*: Nicky, I wonder if you would turn those off . . . I mean, turn *it* off, turn her off, unplug it . . .

(MURRAY *turns the statue off, puts it back into the box.)*

SANDRA: Nicky, when you bought this doll . . .

MURRAY: Sandy, why don't I save you a lot of time. Nick is a fairly bright kid and he knows that girls are *not* boys. Other than that his interest in ladies is confined right now to ones that light up or don't light up.

NICK: I mostly like to read books that are healthy, constructive, and extremely educational for a person.

MURRAY: Don't push it, Nick. He does not have any unusual fixations, Sandy. He is no more abnormally interested in your bust than Mr. Amundson is.

ALBERT: Mr. Burns, it is not necessary to . . .

MURRAY: Of course, I might be wrong about that.

ALBERT: Our interest in that doll . . .

MURRAY: You really *are* interested in that doll, Albert.

ALBERT: Our interest . . .

NICK *(To* ALBERT*)*: I'll sell it to you for two dollars. That's fifty cents less than I paid for it.

(SANDRA *is unable to suppress her amusement and laughs happily.)*

ALBERT *(Quite annoyed with her)*: Sandra, I fail to see . . .

SANDRA *(Controlling herself again, but still smiling)*: It's just that it was funny, Albert.

ALBERT *(Taking command)*: Suppose *I* pursue, then, the psychological part of . . .

SANDRA *(Bristling at him)*: Excuse me, Albert, I really do feel it would be better if *I* were to . . .

MURRAY: Albert, the lady was just laughing because something funny happened. That's actually the best thing to do under the circumstances.

ALBERT: Mr. Burns . . .

MURRAY: How would you all like to go to the Statue of Liberty? I have it on good authority from the Weather Lady that today is a beautiful day.

ALBERT: Is it at all possible, Mr. Burns, for you to stick to the point?

MURRAY: Albert, I bet you'd make Sandy a lot happier if you took her off somewhere once in a while. Doesn't have to be the Statue of Liberty; actually any . . .

ALBERT: My relationship with Dr. Markowitz is of no . . .

MURRAY: Well, there's obviously some relationship. When Nick asked you if you'd have sugar in your coffee before, Albert, you answered for Sandy.

ALBERT: Mr. Burns, this entire interview has reached a point . . .

NICK: I'm going to get my educational books. I left them out on the street.
   (He leaves the apartment, his exit unnoticed by the others.)

ALBERT: This entire interview, Mr. Burns, has . . .

SANDRA: Mr. Burns, I . . .

ALBERT: Damn it, Sandra, don't interrupt me!

SANDRA: Albert, for goodness sakes, you . . .

ALBERT *(Stands up)*: Sandra, perhaps we . . . *(To* MURRAY*)* Would you excuse us for just a moment, Mr. Burns? I'd like to have a short conference with Sandra . . . Miss . . . Dr. Markowitz for a moment. *(She gets up.* ALBERT *and* SANDRA *walk over to the alcove, where* MURRAY *cannot hear them.* MURRAY *starts to peer at them through his binoculars until* ALBERT *turns and looks at him; he then goes to desk and tinkers with clock. Now alone with* SANDRA, ALBERT's *manner changes somewhat. He speaks more softly and with more warmth, a departure from the stiff, professional manner he uses in dealing with* MUR-RAY.*)* Sandra, what are you *doing,* have we lost all control?

SANDRA: Are you seriously talking to *me* about control?

ALBERT: Dear, I told *you* and I told Dr. Malko. It's much too soon for you to go out on cases. You need another year in the office, behind the lines, I told both of you. You're simply *not* ready.

SANDRA: Really, Albert, you hardly let me get started. I was attempting to deal with the whole child.

ALBERT: Three months out of grad school and you want to go right into the front lines. Not advisable.

SANDRA *(Whispering angrily)*: Don't you think that this is rather stupid and unprofessional? Right here in front of him you decide to have a conference.

ALBERT: A necessity. I am supposedly the leader of our examining team . . .

SANDRA: Oh, *really* . . .

ALBERT: You get too *involved,* Sandra. Each case, you get much too emotionally involved. This is an exploratory visit, we are *scientists,* dear, you lose sight of the . . .

SANDRA: You make me sick today, Albert. This is no way to approach this man's problem. We . . .

ALBERT *(sighing)*: Oh, fine. That's fine. Well . . . fine . . .
   *(*MURRAY, *at the other side of the room, picks up a megaphone.)*

MURRAY *(Through the megaphone)*: How are we doing? *(Puts the megaphone down, comes over to them in the alcove, sits between them; speaks sympathetically.*). I personally don't feel that you're gonna work out your problems with each other. But I'm glad you came to me because I think I can help you. Al, Sandy is not going to respect you because you threaten her. Respect will have to come gradually, naturally, a maturing process . . .

ALBERT: Mr. Burns . . .

MURRAY: Sandy, I bet he's got a file on you.

ALBERT: Mr. Burns, according to the B.C.W., the child's continuance in your home is in serious and immediate doubt. I am trying to encourage your cooperation . . . *(He is making a genuine attempt to speak warmly, understandingly.)* Aren't

you at all willing to answer some questions, to give some evidence in your fa-
vour for our report, some evidence to support your competency as a guardian?
The Board is thoroughly aware that Nicholas is not legally adopted.

MURRAY: He's my nephew. He's staying with me for a while. He's visiting.

ALBERT: How long has he been here?

MURRAY: Seven years.

ALBERT: So you see, the Child Welfare Board has, I assure you, the right to question . . .

MURRAY (*Rises, faces* ALBERT *angrily*): You don't assure me of *any*thing, buddy,
you make me damn nervous. Do you mean to tell me that four years at N.Y.U.
has made you my judge? (ALBERT *shrugs, defeated; crosses to Morris chair
for his coat, signals* SANDRA *that they are leaving.* MURRAY *goes toward
them; speaks quietly, apologetically.*). O.K., all right. What do you want to
know? I'll be cooperative.

    (SANDRA *and* ALBERT *sit down again.*)

ALBERT: Nicholas' father, where is he?

MURRAY: That's not a *where* question. That's a *who* question.

ALBERT: I don't quite . . .

MURRAY: Nick's mother, she didn't quite either.

SANDRA: She is still living . . .

MURRAY: My sister is unquestionably alive.

SANDRA: But her responsibility to the child.

MURRAY: For five years she did everything she could for Nick . . . but get married.
Now that's not easy to understand since she used to get married to *everybody.*
But, somehow, having Nick matured her, she felt a responsibility not to get married to just *any*body any more, so she didn't marry Nick's father, nor was she
married at the time he was born. You might call Nick a bastard, or "little bastard," depending on how whimsical you feel at the time. Is that the sort of information you wanted? . . . Ah, this situation is the social workers' paradise. What
a case history, huh? . . . My sister Elaine showed up here one day with two suitcases, a hatbox, a blue parakeet, a dead gold fish, and a five-year-old child.
Three days later she went downstairs to buy a pack of filter-tip cigarettes . . .
(MURRAY *shrugs.*) Six years later she returned for the suitcases and the hatbox . . . the parakeet I had given away, the gold fish I had long since flushed
down the toilet, and the five-year-old child had, with very little effort, become six
years older. When Elaine returned for her luggage I reminded her of the child
and the pack of filter-tip cigarettes and suggested that this was perhaps the longest running practical joke in recent history. She was accompanied by a tall
chap with sunglasses who was born to be her fifth divorce and who tried to start
a small conversation with me. At this point I slapped my sister, Fifth Divorce
slugged me, Sister cried, stopped quite suddenly, and then proceeded to explain to me, briefly, her well-practiced theory on the meaning of life, a philoso-
phy falling somewhere to the left of Whoopie. At which point, I remember, I
started laughing and then we all laughed and said "good-bye" like people at the
end of a long party. That was almost a year ago. And I've still got Nick.

    (SANDRA *is obviously sympathetic to this situation, emotionally involved
in the story;* ALBERT *continues his cool professionalism, here and there
jotting notes in the file.*)

SANDRA: But . . . but I'm sure she must have had *some* concern about Nicholas . . .
about the child . . .

MURRAY: His name is not Nicholas. I will admit that he has stayed with that name much longer than the others . . . no, actually he was "Bill" for almost eight months . . .

SANDRA: I'm sure, on his birth certificate . . .

MURRAY: Certainly an elusive document. Not having given him a last name, Elaine felt reticent about assigning him a first one. When Nick first came here this presented a real difficulty. Nick answered to nothing whatsoever. Even the parakeet recognized its own name. Nick only knew I was calling him when he was positive there was no one else in the room.

SANDRA (*Very much emotionally involved in this now*): Well, how did you communicate with . . .

MURRAY: I made a deal with him when he was six, up to which time he was known rather casually as Chubby, that he could try out any name he wished, for however long he wished, until his thirteenth birthday, at which point he'd have to decide on a name he liked permanently. He went through a long period of dogs' names when he was still little, Rover and King having a real vogue there for a while. For three months he referred to himself as Big Sam, then there was Little Max, Snoopy, Chip, Rock, Rex, Mike, Marty, Lamont, Chevrolet, Wyatt, Yancy, Fred, Phil, Woodrow, Lefty, The Phantom . . . He received his library card last year in the name of Raphael Sabatini, his Cub Scout membership lists him as Barry Fitzgerald, and only last week a friend of his called asking if Toulouse could come over to his house for dinner. Nick seems to be the one that'll stick, though.

SANDRA: His mother . . . ?

MURRAY: His mother, when last heard, was studying mime in Paris, having been given a sort of scholarship by a twenty-two-year-old handbag heir named Myron, who seems to believe strongly in the development of talent and student exchange. Well, I don't believe I've left anything out.

ALBERT: I was not aware that Nick was an O.W. child.

MURRAY: O.W.?

ALBERT: Out of wedlock.

MURRAY: For a moment I thought you meant Prisoner of War. I think it's that natural warmth of yours that leads me to misunderstand.

ALBERT: But as concerns the child . . . (*Looks around the room*) Where is the child?

SANDRA: You preferred not having him here anyway, Albert.

ALBERT (*Sharply*): I am perfectly aware, Sandra, of what I *prefer,* and what I do *not* prefer.

SANDRA (*Sharply*): I don't care for that tone of voice at *all*, Albert.

ALBERT (*Rises, begins to put on his coat; calmly*): Sandra, I understand perfectly what has happened. We have allowed this man to disturb us and we have *both* gotten a bit upset. Now, I really do feel that it's time we got over to that family problem in Queens. It's there in your file, the Ledbetters, the introverted child. We've really given an unreasonable amount of time to this case. This interview, I'm afraid, Mr. Burns, has reached a point . . .

SANDRA (*Attempting to sound authoritative*): Albert, I personally feel that it would not be advisable to leave this particular case, at this point.

ALBERT: Sandra, we have done here this morning all we . . .

SANDRA: I feel that we have not really given Mr. Burns a chance to . . .

ALBERT: Sandra, it's really time we left for Queens . . .

SANDRA (*Hands* ALBERT *one of her two file envelopes*): Here's the Ledbetter file, I'm staying here.

ALBERT (*Raising his voice a little*): Sandra.

SANDRA: I have decided to pursue this case.

ALBERT (*Almost shouting*): Sandra, have we lost all professional control?

SANDRA (*Angry, flustered*): You just . . . you just go yourself to the Leadbellies . . . you go on to Queens.

ALBERT (*Takes her by the arm, gently, but firmly*): May I just talk to you for a moment?

    (ALBERT leads SANDRA over to the alcove.)

MURRY: Time out for signals again?

ALBERT (*Away from* MURRAY, *now he speaks, softly, less stiffly, though still angry*): What *is* this, dear? What has happened to you today? What are you doing?

SANDRA: I'm doing what I think is right.

ALBERT: I know how you feel, Sandra, but there is no more we can do here.

SANDRA (*Emotionally*): I just . . . I just don't understand your behaviour when you're on a case. We're supposed to be of some help, he . . .

ALBERT: Of course I want to help. But don't forget that the child is the one who needs protection, who needs . . .

SANDRA: Are you really going to leave that man here like that? You're not going to even try to help him or tell him what to do about the Board separating him from the child . . . I mean . . . just so cold.

ALBERT (*Takes her hand*): Dear, you spent much too much time at that graduate school and not enough time in the field. That's your whole trouble. You've got to learn your job, Sandra . . .

SANDRA (*Angry, frustrated*): Oh *really,* is that so? Albert Amundson, don't give me any of that nonsense.

ALBERT (*Glancing over at* MURRAY): Please, Sandra . . . dear, this is not the time or the place for . . .

SANDRA (*Shouting*): Graduate school wouldn't have done *you* any harm, Albert, believe *me!* Oh, this is the most terrible thing . . . (*Very close to tears*) You mean . . . you're just going to leave . . .? Do you know what you are . . .? you're a . . . I don't know; . . . but I'll think of something . . .

    (ALBERT walks away, leaving her in the alcove, goes into the main room, calmly picks up his briefcase.)

ALBERT (*Retaining his control, but just a little shaken. To* MURRAY): Mr. Burns . . . You can assume at this point that Miss Markowitz is no longer involved with your case. The Board will be informed that she is no longer involved with this particular case. Her continuing here, to discuss your case . . . at this point . . . is entirely unofficial. You can dismiss any conference . . . that may resume after I leave . . . when I leave here, from your mind. And, regardless of what you think of me . . .

MURRAY: I think you're a dirty O.W.

    (Some of SANDRA's *file papers slip from her hand and fall to the floor.)*

ALBERT: And . . . and do you know what *you* are? (*Readying himself to deliver a crushing insult to* MURRAY) Maladjusted! (*Goes to the door, opens it.*) Good afternoon, Mr. Burns. Good afternoon, Sandra.

MURRAY: Good afternoon, Mr. Amundson. Watch out crossing the street.

    (ALBERT exits, closing door sharply behind him. SANDRA stands for a

moment in the alcove, then begins to pick up the papers she had dropped on the floor.)

SANDRA: Mr. Burns . . . *(She is making a very strong attempt to control herself, but she is obviously on the verge of tears. She goes into the main room, begins to collect her things to leave.)* Mr. Burns, I must apologize to you. We . . . we have put you . . . you have been put at a disadvantage this morning. You have been involved in a personal problem that has nothing to do whatsoever with your particular case. It is entirely wrong for me to give you this impression of our . . . of our profession. *(She can no longer control herself and becomes, suddenly, a sort of child. She stands quite still, with her hands at her sides, and cries. It is not loud, hysterical crying, but intermittent and disorganized sobs, squeaks, whines, sniffles and assorted feminine noises which punctuate her speech.)* Do you know what? I just lost my job. This is awful. He's right, you know. I'm not suited to my work. I get too involved. That's what he said and he's right. *(Rummaging through her purse for Kleenex)* Please don't look at me. Do you *have* to stand there? Please go away. Still, he didn't have to talk to me like that. This is the first *week* we've ever gone on cases together. I didn't think he'd behave that way. That was no way. Why don't I ever have any Kleenex? *(He gives her the closest thing at hand to blow her nose in, his undershirt from the bed.)* Thank you. *(She sits down on the bed.)* Do you know that even with two fellowships it still cost me, I mean my parents mostly, it cost them seven thousand two hundred and forty-five dollars for me to go through school. I was the eighth youngest person to graduate in New York State last year and I can't stop crying. Maybe if I hurry, if I took a cab, I could still meet him in Queens.

MURRAY: You can't. Queens is closed. It's closed for the season.

SANDRA: Do you know what? *(Her crying lets up a bit.)*

MURRAY: What?

SANDRA *(With a new burst of sobs)*: I hate the Ledbetters.

MURRAY: Then I'm sure once I got to know them I'd hate them too.

SANDRA: Mr. Burns, you don't understand. Some of the cases I love and some of them I hate, and that's all wrong for my work, but I can't help it. I hate Raymond Ledbetter and he's only nine years old and he makes me sick and I don't give a damn about him.

MURRAY *(Pointing to the file on her lap)*: You can't like everybody in your portfolio.

SANDRA: But some of them I like too much and worry about them all day . . . *(She is making an attempt to control her tears.)* It is an obvious conflict against all professional standards. I didn't like Raymond Ledbetter so I tried to understand him, and now that I understand him I hate him.

MURRAY: I think that's wonderful. Can I get you a cup of coffee?

SANDRA *(She turns to MURRAY as if to answer him, but instead bursts into fresh tears)*: He's gone to Queens and I'll never hear from him again. I wrote out what my married name would be after dinner last night on a paper napkin, Mrs. Albert Amundson, to see how it would look. You know what I think I am, I think I'm crazy.

MURRAY: Well, then, I can talk to you.

SANDRA: We were going to get married. It was all planned, Mrs. Albert Amundson on a napkin. You have to understand Albert. He's really a very nice person when he's not on cases. He's a very intelligent man but last month I fell asleep twice while he was talking. I've known him for so long. *(She tries once again to stop crying but the effort only increases her sobs.)* Mr. Burns, don't look at me. Why don't you go away?

MURRAY: But I live here.

SANDRA: I would like everybody to go away.

MURRAY *(Attempting to comfort her)*: Can I get you a pastrami sandwich?

SANDRA: Oh, I don't know you and I'm crying right in front of you. Go away.

MURRAY: Couldn't you just think of this as Show-and-Tell time?

SANDRA *(Turning away again, still seated on the bed)*: The minute I got out of school I wanted to go right back inside. *(with a great sob.)* Albert is gone and I just lost my job.

MURRAY *(He walks over to her)*: Now, you're really going to have to stop crying, because I am going out of my mind.

SANDRA: I cry all the time and I laugh in the wrong places in the movies. I am unsuited to my profession and I can't do anything right. Last night I burned an entire chicken and after seven years of school I can't work and I've got no place to go. An entire chicken.

MURRAY: If I do my Peter Lorre imitation, will you stop crying?

SANDRA *(She pokes the file-envelope in her lap)*: Look what I've done, I've cried on one of my files. The ink is running all over the Grumbacher twins . . .

MURRAY *(In the voice of Peter Lorre, a decent imitation):* It was all a mistake, I didn't stab Mrs. Marmalade . . . it was my knife, but someone else did it, I tell you . . .

SANDRA: That's an awful imitation, Mr. Burns . . .

> *(She turns away from him and sobs into the bedclothes. He takes the Bubbles statue out of the box, switches it on, places it on the floor near the bed; it starts to blink on and off. Her face peeks out, she sees the blinking statue and puts her face back into the bedclothes, but we hear some giggles mixing with her sobs now, and then overtaking them, until she finally lifts her face and we see that she is laughing.)*

MURRAY *(Smiling)*: There. Progress. *(He turns off the statue.)* Would you like a cup of coffee, or a pastrami sandwich or something?

SANDRA: No, thank you. (SANDRA *begins to compose herself, she has stopped crying completely and is wiping her eyes with the undershirt he gave her. Then she begins to fold the undershirt neatly, smoothing it out into a nice little square on her lap.)* This is absolutely the most unprofessional experience I have ever had.

MURRAY: People fall into two distinct categories, Miss Markowitz; people who like delicatessen, and people who don't like delicatessen. A man who is not touched by the earthy lyricism of hot pastrami, the pungent fantasy of corned beef, pickles, frankfurters, the great lusty impertinence of good mustard . . . is a man of stone and without heart. Now, Albert is obviously not a lover of delicatessen and you are well rid of him.

> *(SANDRA is still sitting on the bed, her hands folded neatly in her lap on top of her files and his undershirt.)*

SANDRA: What am I going to do? This is an awful day.

MURRAY *(He sits on the swivel chair next to the bed)*: Miss Markowitz, this is a beautiful day and I'll tell you why. My dear, you are really a jolly old girl and you are well rid of Albert. You have been given a rare opportunity to return the unused portion and have your money refunded.

SANDRA: But . . . my work . . . what am I going to . . .

MURRAY: You are a lover, Dr. Markowitz, you are a lover of things and people so you took up work where you could get at as many of them as possible; and it just turned out that there were too many of them and too much that moves you. Damn it, please be glad that it turned out you are not reasonable and sensible. Have all the gratitude you can, that you are capable of embarrassment and joy and are a marathon crier.

SANDRA *(Looking directly at him)*: There is a kind of relief that it's gone . . . the job, and even Albert. But I know what it is, it's just irresponsible. . . . I don't have the vaguest idea who I am. . . .

MURRAY *(He takes her hand)*: It's just there's all these Sandras running around who you never met before, and it's confusing at first, fantastic, like a Chinese fire drill. But god *damn,* isn't it great to find out how many Sandras there are? Like those little cars in the circus, this tiny red car comes out and putters around, suddenly its doors open and out come a thousand clowns, whooping and hollering and raising hell.

SANDRA *(She lets go of his hand in order to pick up the undershirt in her lap)*: What's this?

MURRAY: That's my undershirt. How's about going to the Empire State Building with me?

SANDRA: I'll have that coffee now.

MURRAY: You didn't answer my question. Would you like to visit the Empire State Building?

SANDRA: No, not really.

MURRAY: Well, then how about the zoo?

SANDRA: Not just now.

MURRAY: Well, then will you marry me?

SANDRA: What?

MURRAY: Just a bit of shock treatment there. I have found after long experience that it's the quickest way to get a woman's attention when her mind wanders. Always works.

SANDRA: Mr. Burns . . .

MURRAY: Now that you've cried you can't call me Mr. Burns. Same rule applies to laughing. My name is Murray.

SANDRA: Well, Murray, to sort of return to reality for a minute . . .

MURRAY: I will only go as a tourist.

SANDRA: Murray, you know, you're in trouble with the Child Welfare Board. They could really take Nick away. Murray, there's some things you could try to do . . . to make your case a little stronger . . .

MURRAY: Sandra, do you realize that you are not wearing your shoes?

SANDRA *(She looks down at her bare feet)*: Oh.

(The front door opens and NICK *bursts into the room, laden with books.)*

NICK: Well, here I am with all my favourite books, *Fun in the Rain, The Young Railroader, Great Philosophers, Science for Youth,* a Spanish dictionary. What I did was I left them out in the street when I was playing, and I went down to . . .

MURRAY: Nick, you just killed a month's allowance for nothing. Miss Markowitz isn't even on our case any more.

NICK: I shouldn't have left. You got angry and insulted everybody.

MURRAY: Don't worry about it, Nick, we'll work it out. *(He goes over to the closet for something.)*

NICK *(Dropping his books regretfully on the chair)*: Four dollars right out the window. *(To* SANDRA*)* Y'know, I really do read educational books and am encouraged in my home to think.

SANDRA: I'm sure that's true, Nicholas, but I'm not in a position to do you much official good any more.

NICK: We're in real trouble now, right? *(He turns to* MURRAY *who has taken two ukuleles from the closet and is coming toward* NICK.*)* I figured it would happen; you got angry and hollered at everybody.

MURRAY: Nick, we have a guest, a music lover. . . . *(He hands the smaller of the two ukuleles to* NICK.*)* We've got to do our song. I am sure it will be requested.

NICK *(Protesting, gesturing with his ukulele)*: Murray, stop it . . . we—this is no time to sing songs, Murray. . . .

MURRAY *(Striking a downbeat on his ukulele)*: Come on, where's your professional attitude?

> *(MURRAY starts playing "Yes, Sir, That's My Baby" on the ukulele, then sings the first line. NICK turns away at first, shaking his head solemnly at MURRAY's behaviour. MURRAY goes on with the second line of the song. Reluctantly, NICK begins to pick out the melody on his ukulele, then he smiles in spite of himself and sings the third line along with MURRAY.*
>
> *They really go into the song now, singing and playing "Yes, Sir, That's My Baby," doing their routine for SANDRA. She sits in front of them on the bed, smiling, enjoying their act. NICK is in the spirit of it now and having a good time. In the middle of the song NICK and MURRAY do some elaborate soft-shoe dance steps for a few lines, ukuleles held aloft. This is followed by some very fast and intricate two-part ukulele harmony on the last few lines of the song for a big finish.*
>
> *SANDRA applauds.*
>
> *MURRAY and NICK, singing and strumming ukes, go into a reprise of the song, MURRAY moving forward and sitting down on the bed next to SANDRA. NICK, left apart from them now, does a line or two more of the song along with MURRAY, then gradually stops. NICK considers them both for a moment as MURRAY goes on doing the song alone now for SANDRA. NICK nods to himself, circles around in front of them and, unnoticed by them, puts his uke down on the window seat, goes to his alcove, gets school briefcase and pajamas from his bed. MURRAY is still playing the uke and singing the song to SANDRA as NICK goes past them on his way to the front door, carrying his stuff.)*

NICK *(Pleasantly, to* SANDRA*)*: Nice to meet you, lady, I'll see you around.

MURRAY *(Stops singing, turns to* NICK*)*: Where you off to, Nick?

NICK: Gonna leave my stuff up at Mrs. Myers'. *(Opens the door.)* I figure I'll be staying over there tonight.

> *(NICK exits, waving a pleasant good-bye to SANDRA. SANDRA looks at the front door, puzzled; then she looks at MURRAY, who resumes the song, singing and strumming the uke.)*
>
> *Curtain*

ACT TWO

Scene: MURRAY's *apartment, eight A.M. the following morning.*

At rise: The phone is ringing loudly on the window seat. MURRAY *enters from the bathroom with his toothbrush in his mouth, grabs the phone. The room is as it was at the end of Act One except that there is a six-foot-high folding screen placed around the bed, hiding it from view, and the shades are drawn again on the windows.*

MURRAY *(Speaks immediately into the phone)*: Is this somebody with good news or money? No? Good-bye. *(He hangs up.)* It's always voices like that you hear at eight A.M. Maniacs. *(He pulls up the shade to see what kind of a day it is outside. As usual the lighting of the room changes not at all with the shade up, as before he sees nothing but the blank, grayish wall opposite.)* Crap. *(With a sigh of resignation, he picks up the phone, dials, listens.)* Hello, Weather Lady. I am fine, how are you? What is the weather? Uh-huh . . . uh-huh . . . uh-huh . . . very nice. Only a *chance* of showers? Well, what exactly does that . . . Aw, there she goes again . . . *(He hangs up.)* Chance of showers. *(The phone rings. He picks it up, speaks immediately into it.)* United States Weather Bureau forecast for New York City and vicinity: eight A.M. temperature, sixty-five degrees, somewhat cooler in the suburbs, cloudy later today with a chance of . . . *(Looks incredulously at the phone.)* He hung up. Fool. Probably the most informative phone call he'll make all day. *(He stands, opens the window, leans out, raising his voice, shouting out the window.)* This is your neighbour speaking! Something must be done about your garbage cans in the alley here. It is definitely second-rate garbage! By next week I want to see a better class of garbage, more empty champagne bottles and caviar cans! So let's *snap* it up and get on the *ball!*
    (SANDRA's head appears at the top of the screen, like a puppet's head. She is staring blankly at MURRAY. MURRAY steps toward her, she continues to stare blankly at him. Her head suddenly disappears again behind the screen. The screen masks the entire bed and SANDRA from his view, and the view of audience. We hear a rustle of sheets and blankets, silence for a couple of seconds, and then SANDRA's voice; she speaks in a cold, dignified, ladylike voice, only slightly tinged with sleep, impersonal, polite, and distant, like one unintroduced party guest to another.)
SANDRA: Good morning.
MURRAY: Good morning.
SANDRA: How are you this morning?
MURRAY: I am fine this morning. How are you?
SANDRA: I am fine also. Do you have a bathrobe?
MURRAY: Yes, I have a bathrobe.
SANDRA: May I have your bathrobe, please?
MURRAY: I'll give you Nick's. It'll fit you better.
SANDRA: That seems like a good idea. *(He takes NICK's bathrobe from the hook in the alcove, tosses it over the top of the screen.)*
MURRAY: There you go.
SANDRA *(Her voice from behind the screen is getting even colder)*: Thank you. What time is it?
MURRAY: It is eight-fifteen and there is a chance of showers. Did you sleep well?

SANDRA: Yes. How long have you been up?

MURRAY: Little while.

SANDRA: Why didn't you wake me?

MURRAY: Because you were smiling. *(Silence for a moment)* How does the bathrobe fit?

SANDRA: This bathrobe fits fine. *(After a moment.)* Did you happen to see my clothes?

MURRAY *(Starts for the bathroom)*: They're in the bathroom. Shall I get them?

SANDRA: No, thank you. *(She suddenly pops out from behind the screen and races across the room into the kitchen at right, slamming the kitchen door behind her. We hear her voice from behind the door.)* This isn't the bathroom. This is the kitchen.

MURRAY: If it *was* the bathroom then this would be a very extreme version of an efficiency apartment. *(He goes to the bathroom to get her clothes, brings them with him to the kitchen door. He knocks on the door.)* Here are your clothes. Also toothpaste and toothbrush.

    (The kitchen door opens slightly, her hand comes out. He puts the stuff in it, her hand goes back, the door closes again.)

SANDRA: Thank you.

MURRAY: Sandy, is everything all right?

SANDRA: What?

MURRAY: I said, is everything all right?

SANDRA: Yes. I'm using the last of your toothpaste.

MURRAY: That's all right. There's soap by the sink.

SANDRA: I know. I found it.

MURRAY: That's good.

SANDRA: It was right by the sink.

MURRAY: Suppose we broaden this discussion to other matters . . .

SANDRA: I saw the soap when I came in.

    (The front door opens and ARNOLD BURNS enters as he did before, carrying a grocery carton filled with varieties of fruit. He sets it down on the desk.)

ARNOLD: Morning, Murray.

MURRAY *(Without turning to look at him)*: Morning, Arnold.

ARNOLD: Murray, Chuckles called again yesterday. I told him I'd talk to you. And Jimmy Sloan is in from the coast; he's putting a new panel-show package together . . .

MURRAY: Arnold, you have many successful clients . . .

ARNOLD: Murray . . .

MURRAY: With all these successful people around, where are all of our new young failures going to come from?

ARNOLD: Murray, those people I saw here yesterday; they were from the Welfare Board, right? I tried to warn you . . .

MURRAY: Nothing to worry about.

ARNOLD: These Welfare people don't kid around.

MURRAY: Arnold, I don't mind you coming with fruit if you keep quiet, but you bring a word with every apple . . . Everything's fine. You'll be late for the office.

ARNOLD: Is Nick all right?

MURRAY: Fine.

ARNOLD: O.K., good-bye, Murray.

MURRAY: Good-bye, Arnold. *(ARNOLD exits. MURRAY talks to the closed kitchen door again.)* There's coffee still in the pot from last night, if you want to heat it up.

SANDRA: I already lit the flame.

MURRAY: Good. The cups are right over the sink. Will you be coming out soon?

SANDRA: Yes, I think so. Cream and sugar in your coffee?

MURRAY: Yes, thank you.

SANDRA: Murray.

MURRAY: Yes.

SANDRA: I'm coming out now.

MURRAY: That's good.

SANDRA: I'm all finished in here so I'm coming out now.

MURRAY: That's very good.

> *(The kitchen door opens. SANDRA, dressed neatly, comes out of the kitchen, carrying two cups of coffee and NICK's bathrobe.)*

SANDRA *(Pausing at kitchen doorway, smiles politely)*: Well, here I am. *(She goes to MURRAY, gives him a cup, sits on swivel chair. He sits next to her, on the stool. She takes a sip of coffee, straightens her hair. She is quite reserved, though pleasant; she behaves as though at a tea social.)* You know, yesterday was the first time I've ever been to the Statue of Liberty. It's funny how you can live in a city for so long and not visit one of its most fascinating sights.

MURRAY: That is funny. *(He sips his coffee.)* This coffee isn't bad, for yesterday's coffee.

SANDRA: I think it's very good, for yesterday's coffee. *(Takes another sip.)* What kind of coffee is it?

MURRAY: I believe it's Chase and Sanborn coffee.

SANDRA: "Good to the last drop," isn't that what they say?

MURRAY: I think that's Maxwell House.

SANDRA: Oh yes. Maxwell House coffee. "Good to the last drop."

MURRAY: It's Chase and Sanborn that used to have the ad about the ingredients: "Monizalles for mellowness" was one.

SANDRA: They used to sponsor Edgar Bergen and Charlie McCarthy on the radio.

MURRAY: Yes. You're right.

SANDRA: "Monizalles for mellowness." I remember. That's right. *(She finishes her coffee, puts her cup down on the table. Then, after a moment)* I have to leave now.

MURRAY: Oh?

SANDRA: Yes. I'll have to be on my way. *(She stands, takes her pocketbook, puts on her shoes and starts to exit.)*

MURRAY *(Takes her files from the floor, hands them to her)*: Don't forget your files.

SANDRA: Oh yes. My files. *(She takes them from him, stands looking at him.)* Well, good-bye.

MURRAY: Good-bye, Sandra.

SANDRA: Good-bye. *(She walks out of the apartment, and closes the door behind her. Alone in the apartment now, MURRAY stands for a moment looking at the door. He then runs to open the door; she has had her hand on the outside knob and is dragged into the room as he does so.)*

MURRAY *(laughing, relieved)*: You nut. I was ready to kill you.

SANDRA *(Throws her arms around him, drops her bag and files on floor)*: What happened? You didn't say anything. I was waiting for you to say something. Why didn't you say something or kiss me or . . .

MURRAY: I was waiting for *you,* for God's sake. *(He kisses her.)*

SANDRA: I didn't know *what* was going on. *(She kisses him, their arms around each other; he leans away from her for a moment to put his coffee cup on the table.)* Don't let me go . . .

MURRAY: I was just putting my coffee cup down . . .

SANDRA: Don't let me go. *(He holds her tightly again.)* Murray, I thought about it, and I probably love you.

MURRAY: That's very romantic. I probably love you too. You have very small feet. For a minute yesterday, it looked like you only had four toes, and I thought you were a freak. I woke up in the middle of the night and counted them. There are five.

SANDRA: I could have told you that.

MURRAY *(He sits in the swivel chair; she is on his lap)*: You knocked down maybe seven boxes of Crackerjacks yesterday. You are twelve years old. You sleep with the blanket under your chin like a napkin. When you started to talk about the coffee before, I was going to throw you out the window except there'd be no place for you to land but the trash can from the Chinese restaurant.

SANDRA: You mean that you live above a Chinese restaurant?

MURRAY: Yes. It's been closed for months, though.

SANDRA: Do you mean that you live above an abandoned Chinese restaurant?

MURRAY: Yes, I do.

SANDRA: That's wonderful. *(She kisses him; jumps up from his lap happily excited about what she has to say. Takes off her jacket and hangs it on the back of the Morris chair.)* I didn't go to work this morning and I simply can't tell you how fantastic that makes me feel. I'm not going to do a *lot* of things any more. *(Picks at the material of her blouse.)* This blouse I'm wearing, my mother picked it out, everybody picks out things for me. She gets all her clothes directly from Louisa May Alcott. *(Picks up the stool, changes its position in the room.)* Well, we've all seen the last of this blouse anyway. Do you realize that I feel more at home here after twenty-four hours than I do in my parents' house after twenty-five years? Of course, we'll have to do something about curtains . . . and I hope you didn't mind about the screen around the bed, I just think it gives such a nice, separate bedroomy effect to that part of the room . . . *(Picks up her bag and files from the floor where she dropped them, puts them in the closet. She is moving in.)* Oh, there are so many wonderful tricks you can try with a one-room apartment, really, if you're willing to use your imagination . . . *(He watches helplessly as she moves happily about the apartment judging it with a decorator's eye.)* I don't care if it sounds silly, Murray, but I was projecting a personality identification with the Statue of Liberty yesterday . . . courageous and free and solid metal . . . *(She kisses him, then continues pacing happily.)* I was here with you last night and I don't give a damn who knows it or what anybody thinks, and that goes for Dr. Malko, Albert, my mother, Aunt Blanche . . . Oh, I'm going to do so many things I've always wanted to do.

MURRAY: For example.

SANDRA: Well . . . I'm not sure right now. And that's marvelous too, I am thoroughly enjoying the idea that I don't know what I'm going to do next. *(Stops pacing.)* Do you have an extra key?

MURRAY: What?

SANDRA: An extra key. Altman's has this terrific curtain sale, thought I'd go and . . .

MURRAY: Well, then I'd better give you some money . . .

SANDRA: No, that's all right. *(Holds out her hand.)* Just the key.

MURRAY: Oh. *(He looks at her blankly for a moment, then reaches into his pocket slowly, finds the key, slowly hands it to her.)*

SANDRA *(Snatches up the key, goes on delightedly pacing up and down)*: Murray, did we bring back any Crackerjacks?

MURRAY *(Pointing to some packages on the desk)*: Only stuff we brought back was that cleaning equipment. I'll admit this place is a little dirty, but all that stuff just for . . .

(The doorbell rings. SANDRA flinches for a moment, but then smiles and stands firmly.)

SANDRA: You'd better answer it, Murray.

MURRAY: Sandra, would you prefer to . . .

(He indicates the kitchen as a hiding place, but she stands right where she is, refusing to move.)

SANDRA: I've got no reason to hide from anybody.

(MURRAY goes to the front door and opens it halfway, but enough for us to see the visitor, ALBERT AMUNDSON. ALBERT cannot see beyond the door to where SANDRA is standing.)

ALBERT: Good morning, Mr. Burns.

MURRAY: Albert, how are you?

(SANDRA, hearing ALBERT's voice, and realizing who it is, goes immediately into the closet, closing the door behind her.)

ALBERT: May I come in?

MURRAY: Sure.

(MURRAY opens the front door all the way, allowing ALBERT into the main room. MURRAY closes the door, then follows ALBERT into the room. MURRAY smiles to himself when he sees that SANDRA is not there and then glances at the closet door.)

ALBERT: I called you twice this morning, Mr. Burns.

MURRAY: That was you.

ALBERT: That was me. Miss Markowitz did not show up in Queens yesterday.

MURRAY: So?

ALBERT: Her parents are quite upset. I am quite upset. Where is she?

MURRAY: She's hiding in the closet.

ALBERT: We're really all quite anxious to know where she is.

MURRAY: I'm not kidding. She's in the closet.

(ALBERT goes to the closet, opens the door, sees SANDRA, then closes the door. ALBERT comes back to MURRAY.)

ALBERT: She *is* in the closet.

MURRAY: I wouldn't lie to you, Albert.

ALBERT: Why is she in the closet?

MURRAY: I don't know. She's got this thing about closets.

ALBERT: That's a very silly thing for her to be in the closet.

MURRAY: Don't knock it till you've tried it. Now, what else can I do for you?

ALBERT: That's a difficult thing for me to believe. I mean, that she's right there in the closet. You are not a person, Mr. Burns, you are an experience.

MURRAY *(Goes into the kitchen)*: That's very nice, Albert, I'll have to remember that.

ALBERT: Actually, Dr. Markowitz is not the reason for my visit today. I came here in an official capacity.

MURRAY *(From the kitchen)*: You don't wear an official capacity well, Albert. Coffee?

ALBERT: No, thank you.

> *(MURRAY brings the pot out, fills the two cups on the table; brings one of the cups of coffee to the closet and hands it through the partly open door.)*

MURRAY *(Returns to the table, sits opposite* ALBERT): What have you got on your mind, Albert?

ALBERT *(Sits; begins hesitantly)*: Burns, late yesterday afternoon the Child Welfare Board made a decision on your case. Their decision is based on three months of a thorough study; our interview yesterday is only a small part of the . . . I want you to understand that I am not responsible, personally, for the decision they've reached, I . . .

MURRAY: Relax, Albert, I won't even hold you responsible for the shadow you're throwing on my rug.

ALBERT: For eleven months you have avoided contact with the Board, made a farce of their inquiries. You are not employed, show no inclination to gain employment, have absolutely no financial stability . . .

MURRAY: Look, Albert, I . . .

ALBERT: Months of research by the Board and reports by the Revere School show a severe domestic instability, a libertine self-indulgence, a whole range of circumstances severely detrimental to the child's welfare . . .

MURRAY: Look, stop the tap-dancing for a second, Albert; what's going on, what . . .

ALBERT: It is the Board's decision that you are unfit to be the guardian of your nephew, and that action be taken this Friday to remove the child from this home and the deprivation you cause him.

MURRAY: You mean they can really . . . *(Sips his coffee, putting on an elaborate display of calm, showing no emotion.)* Where'd they get this routine from, Charles Dickens?

ALBERT: The Board is prepared to find a more stable, permanent home for your nephew, a family with whom he will live a more wholesome, normal . . .

MURRAY: Look, Albert, there must be some kind of a hearing or something, where I'll have a chance to . . .

ALBERT: You will have the opportunity Thursday to state your case to the Board. If there is some substantial change in your circumstances, some evidence they're not aware of; if you can demonstrate that you are a responsible member of society . . .

MURRAY: It's Tuesday; what the hell am I supposed to do in two days, win the Nobel Peace Prize? They sent you here to tell me this?

ALBERT: No, you were to be informed by the court. But in view of the confusion which took place here yesterday, for which I consider myself responsible, I felt it my duty to come here and explain . . .

MURRAY: Buddy, you speak like you write everything down before you say it.

ALBERT: Yes, I do speak that way, Mr. Burns. I wish that I spoke more spontaneously. I realize that I lack warmth. I will always appear foolish in a conversation with a person of your imagination. Please understand, there is no vengeance in my activities here. I love my work, Mr. Burns. I believe that you are a danger to this child. I wish this were not true, because it is obvious that you have considerable affection for your nephew. It is in your face, this feeling. I admire you for your warmth, Mr. Burns, and for the affection the child feels for you. I admire this because I am one for whom children do not easily feel affection. I am not one of the warm people. But your feeling for the child does not mollify the genuinely dangerous emotional climate you have made for him. *(He moves toward* MURRAY.*)* I wish you could understand this, I would so much rather you understood, could really hear what I have to say. For yours is, I believe, a distorted picture of this world.

MURRAY: Then why don't you send *me* to a foster home?

ALBERT: I was right. You really can't listen to me. You are so sure of your sight. Your villains and heroes are all so terribly clear to you, and I am obviously one of the villains. *(Picks up his briefcase.)* God save you from your vision, Mr. Burns. *(Goes to the front door, opens it.)* Good-bye. (ALBERT *exits.)*

MURRAY *(Stands at the window with his coffee cup in his hand, looking out at gray, blank wall of the building opposite)*: Hey, courageous, free one, you can come out now.

(SANDRA *comes out of closet carrying her coffee cup;* MURRAY *does not look at her.)*

SANDRA: I'm sorry, Murray. I'm really very embarrassed. I don't know what happened. I just ran into the closet. And . . . and once I was in there, I just didn't want to come out. I'm sorry, Murray . . .

MURRAY: Don't be nervous, lady, you're just going through an awkward stage. You're between closets. *(Quietly, calmly)* Look, if Nick has to leave, if he goes, he goes, and my life stays about the same. But it's no good for *him,* see, not for a couple of years, anyway. Right now he's still ashamed of being sharper than everybody else, he could easily turn into another peeled and boiled potato. Are you listening to me?

SANDRA: Yes, of course . . .

MURRAY: Well, make some kind of listening noise then, will you? Wink or nod your head or something.

SANDRA: But, I'm . . .

MURRAY *(Casually; gesturing with his coffee cup)*: Tell you the truth, it's even a little better for me if he goes. I mean, he's a middle-aged kid. When I signed with the network he sat up all night figuring out the fringe benefits and the pension plan. And he started to make *lists* this year. Lists of everything; subway stops, underwear, what he's gonna do next week. If somebody doesn't watch out he'll start making lists of what he's gonna do next year and the next ten years. Hey, suppose they put him in with a whole family of listmakers? *(Angrily)* I didn't spend six years with him so he should turn into a listmaker. He'll learn to know everything before it happens, he'll learn to plan, he'll learn how to be one of the nice dead people. Are you listening?

SANDRA: Of course, I told you, Murray, I . . .

MURRAY: Then stamp your feet or mutter so I'll know you're there, huh? *(Still speaking quite calmly)* I just want him to stay with me till I can be sure he won't turn into Norman Nothing. I want to be sure he'll know when he's chickening out on himself. I want him to get to know exactly the special thing he is or else he won't notice it when it starts to go. I want him to stay awake and know who the phonies are, I want him to know how to holler and put up an argument, I want a little guts to show before I can let him go. I want to be sure he sees all the wild possibilities. I want him to know it's worth all the trouble just to give the world a little goosing when you get the chance. And I want him to know the subtle, sneaky, important reason why he was born a human being and not a chair. *(Pause)* I will be very sorry to see him go. That kid was the best straight man I ever had. He is a laugher, and laughers are rare. I mean, you tell that kid something funny . . . not just any piece of corn, but something funny, and he'll give you your money's worth. It's not just funny jokes he reads, or I tell him, that he laughs at. Not just set-up funny stuff. He sees street jokes, he has the good eye, he sees subway farce and crosstown-bus humour and all the cartoons that people make by being alive. He has a good eye. And I don't want him to leave until I'm certain he'll never be ashamed of it. *(Still quite calmly, unemotionally)* And in addition to that . . . besides that . . . see *(Suddenly; loudly)* Sandy, I don't want him to go. I like having him around here. What should I do, Sandy? Help me out. *(Suddenly slumps forward in his chair, covers his face with his hands; very quietly)* I like when he reads me from the want ads.

SANDRA *(Takes his hands)*: Murray, don't worry, we'll do something. I know the Board, their procedure, there's things you can do . . .

MURRAY *(Quietly, thoughtfully):* What I'll do is I'll buy a new suit. The first thing is to get a dignified suit.

SANDRA: If you could get some kind of a job, get your brother to help you.

MURRAY: Right. Right.

SANDRA: Is there something you can get in a hurry?

MURRAY: Sure, one of those suits with the ready-made cuffs . . .

SANDRA: No, I mean a job. If we could just bring some proof of employment to the hearing, Murray, show them how anxious you are to change. We'll show them you want to be reliable.

MURRAY *(Brightening)*: Yeah, reliable . . . *(Rises; going toward the phone)* Sandy, we will put on a God-damned show for them. Spectacular reliability; a reliability parade; bands, floats, everything. *(Starts to dial.)* Sandy, go to the files and pick me out a tie that is quiet but at the same time projects a mood of inner strength. *(Into the phone)* Arnold Burns' office, please.

SANDRA *(On her way to the file cabinet)*: One quiet tie with a mood of inner strength.

MURRAY *(Into the phone)*: Hello, Margot? It's Murray. Oh, well, when Arnie comes in here's what you do. First you tell him to sit down. Then you tell him I want to get a job. When he has recovered sufficiently from that shock, tell him . . . *(SANDRA comes to him with a tie.)* Excuse me a second, Margot . . .*(To SANDRA, indicating the tie)* Yes, quiet but with strength. *(SANDRA laughs.)* Sandy, that is the greatest happy laugh I ever heard on a lady. Do that again. *(She laughs again.)* Great. Keep that laugh. I'll need it later. *(Into the phone)* Margot, tell him I'm going downtown to pick up a new suit for myself and a beautiful pineapple for him, call him back in about an hour, O.K.? Thanks, Margot. *(Puts the phone down, goes to get his jacket.)*

SANDRA: Can I come with you? I'd love to buy a suit with you.

MURRAY *(Putting on his jacket)*: Better not, Sandy. Gotta move fast. These shoes look O.K.? *(She nods, he takes her hand.)* Look, don't go away.

SANDRA: I won't. *(She kisses him.)*

MURRAY *(Goes to the front door; turns to her, smiles)*: Say "Good luck."

SANDRA: Good luck.

MURRAY *(Opening the door)*: Now say "You are a magnificent human being."

SANDRA: You are a magnificent human being.

MURRAY *(As he exits)*: I *thought* you'd notice.

> *She stands in door and watches him go as the lights fade out quickly. Immediately, as the lights fade, we hear the voice of Chuckles the Chipmunk (LEO HERMAN).*

LEO'S VOICE: Hi there, kidderoonies; there's nothin' more lonelier than a lonely, little looney Chippermunk. So won't ya please come on along with me fer a fun hour, 'cuz that loneliest, littlest, looniest Chippermunk, is *me* . . . Chuckles. *(Lights come up now in ARNOLD BURNS' office, later that afternoon. The office is part of a large theatrical agency of which ARNOLD is a rather successful member; modern, wood panelling, nonobjective paintings and framed photographs of his clients on the wall, a spectacularly large window behind the desk with a twenty-second-floor skyline view. A large bowl of fruit is on an end table near the door. One of the two phones on ARNOLD's desk is a special speakerphone, consisting of a small loudspeaker box on the desk which amplifies clearly the voice of whoever is calling. It can also be spoken into from almost any point in the room if one is facing it. As the following scene progresses the speaker-phone is treated by those present as if it were a person in the room, they gesture to it, smile at it. ARNOLD is alone in his office, leaning against his desk, listening to the speaker-phone, from which we continue to hear the voice of LEO HERMAN.)* God damn it, Arn; that's the intro Murray wrote for me two *years* ago, and it's still lovely, still warm. It's the way the kids know me, the way I say "Hello, kids"; he's a sweetie of a writer.

ARNOLD: That was *last* year he won the sweetie award, Leo.

LEO'S VOICE *(Laughs good-naturedly)*: Please excuse my little words. They slip out of my face once in a while. Arn, you got my voice comin' out of that speakerphone in your office, huh? Comes out like the biggest phony you ever met, right? That's how I sound, don't I? Big phony.

ARNOLD: No, Leo.

LEO'S VOICE: I'm getting sick of myself. Hey, Arn, you figure there's a good chance of Murray comin' back with me on the show?

ARNOLD: Can't guarantee it, Leo; I've sent him to one other appointment today, fairly good offer . . .

LEO'S VOICE: Well, I'm hopin' he comes back with *me,* Arn. Funny bit you being the agent for your own brother—what d'ya call that?

ARNOLD: It's called incest. *(The intercom buzzes; ARNOLD picks it up.)* O.K., send him in. *(Into the speaker-phone)* Got a call, fellah; check back with you when Murray shows.

LEO'S VOICE: Right, 'bye now.

> *(MURRAY enters wearing a new suit and carrying a beautiful pineapple.)*

MURRAY: Good afternoon, Mr. Burns.

ARNOLD: Good afternoon, Mr. Burns. Hey, you really did get a new suit, didn't you? How'd the appointment go with . . .

MURRAY *(Putting the pineapple on the desk, gestures around at the office)*. Arnold, every time I see you, the agency's put you on a higher floor. I swear, next time I come you'll be up in a balloon.

ARNOLD: Murray, the appointment . . .

MURRAY: Can't get over this office, Arnie. *(Goes to the window, looks out.)* Twenty-second floor. You can see everything *(Shocked by something he sees out of the window.)* My God. I don't believe it: it's King Kong. He's sitting on top of the Time-Life Building. He . . . he seems to be crying. Poor gorilla bastard, they shoulda told him they don't make those buildings the way they used to . . .

ARNOLD *(Raising his hand in the air)*: Hello, Murray, hello there . . . here we are in my office. Welcome to Tuesday. Now, come *on,* how'd it go with Jimmy Sloan?

MURRAY: He took me to lunch at Stefanos, East Fifty-third. Christ, it's been a coupla years since I hustled around lunchland. There is this crazy hum that I haven't heard for so long, Arnie; eight square yards of idea men, busily having ideas, eating away at their chef's salad like it's Crackerjacks and there's a prize at the bottom.

ARNOLD: And Sloan . . .?

MURRAY *(Sitting on the sofa)*: Sloan lunches beautifully, can out-lunch anybody. He used to be a Yes-man but he got himself some guts and now he goes around bravely saying "maybe" to everybody. And a killer, this one, Arnie; notches on his attaché case. Told me this idea he had where I'd be a lovable eccentric on his panel show. This somehow led him very logically to his conception of God, who he says is "probably a really fun guy."

ARNOLD: What'd you tell him about the offer?

MURRAY: I told him good-bye. I don't think he noticed when I left; he focuses slightly to the right of you when he talks, just over your shoulder, so if you stay out of range he can't tell that you're gone. Probably thinks I'm still there.

ARNOLD: Murray, you told me this morning to get any job I could; Sloan's offer wasn't so bad . . .

MURRAY: Sloan is an idiot.

ARNOLD *(Sitting next to him on the sofa; angrily, firmly)*: Listen, cookie, I got *news* for you, right now you *need* idiots. You got a bad reputation for quitting jobs; I even had trouble grabbing Sloan for you. Why did you have to go and build your own personal blacklist; why couldn't you just be blacklisted as a Communist like everybody else?

MURRAY: Don't worry, Arnie; I figured I'd go back with Chuckles. He's ready to take me back, isn't he?

ARNOLD: Yea, he's ready. I just spoke to him. *(Solemnly)* Hey, Murray, Leo says he came up to your place last January, a week after you quit him, to talk you into coming back with the show. And right in the middle you went into the kitchen and started singing "Yes, Sir, That's My Baby." Just left him standing there. Your way of saying "good-bye."

MURRAY: Well, that was five months ago, Arnie . . .

ARNOLD *(Attempts to conceal his amusement, then turns to MURRAY, smiling)*: So, what'd you do with him, just left him standing there? *(He laughs.)* Like to have been there, seen that, must have been great.

MURRAY: Arnie, it was beautiful.

ARNOLD *(Still laughing)*: It's about time somebody left Leo Herman standing around talking to himself. *(Rubbing his head)* I wish to God I didn't enjoy you so much. Crap, I don't do you any good at all. *(Then, solemnly again.)* Murray, no fun and games with Leo today, understand? He is absolutely *all* we got left before the hearing Thursday.

MURRAY: Yes, I understand.

ARNOLD *(Goes to pick up the phone on the desk)*: I wish we coulda got something better for you, kid, but there just wasn't any time.

MURRAY: Well, Chuckles won't be so bad for a while . . .

ARNOLD: No, Murray. *(Puts phone down firmly.)* Not just for a while. You'll really have to stick with Chuckles. I had our agency lawyer check the facts for me. Most the Board'll will give you is a probationary year with Nick; a trial period. The Board's investigators will be checking on you every week . . .

MURRAY: That's charming.

ARNOLD: . . . checking to see if you've still got the job, checking with Leo on your stability, checking up on the change in your home environment.

MURRAY: Sounds like a parole board.

ARNOLD *(Into the intercom phone)*: Margot; get me Leo Herman on the speaker-phone here, his home number. Thanks. *(Puts the phone down.)* He's waiting for our call. Look, Murray, maybe he's not the greatest guy in the world; but y'know, he really *likes* you, Murray, he . . .

MURRAY: Yeah. I have a way with animals.

ARNOLD *(Pointing at MURRAY)*: That was your last joke for today. *(A click is heard from speaker-phone; ARNOLD turns it on.)* You there, Leo?

LEO'S VOICE: Right, Arn. I'm down here in the basement, in my gymnasium; lot of echoing. Am I coming through, am I coming through O.K.?

ARNOLD: Clearly, Leo. Murray's here.

LEO'S VOICE: Murray! Murray the wonderful wild man; fellah, how are ya?

MURRAY *(Takes his hat off, waves hello to the speaker-phone)*: O.K., Leo, how're you doing?

LEO'S VOICE: Oh, you crazy bastard, it's damn good to hear that voice again. You're an old monkey, aren't ya?

MURRAY: You sound about the same too, Leo.

LEO'S VOICE: Not the same. I'm *more impossible* than I used to be. Can you imagine that?

MURRAY: Not easily, Leo; no.

LEO'S VOICE: Murray, I need you, fellah; I need you back with the show. Murr', we'll talk a while now, and then I'll come over to your place tonight, go over some ideas for next week's shows. It'll be great, sweetie . . . Oh, there's that word again. "Sweetie," I said that word again. Oh, am I getting *sick* of myself. Big phony. The truth, fellah, I'm the biggest phony you ever met, right?

MURRAY: Probably, Leo.

LEO'S VOICE *(After a pause; coldly)*: Probably, he says. There he goes, there goes Murray the old joker, right? You're a jester, right? Some fooler. You can't fool with a scheduled show, Murray; a scheduled show with a tight budget. *(Softly, whispering)* Murray, come closer, tell you a secret . . . *(MURRAY comes closer to the box.)* You're gonna hate me, Murray; I gotta tell you something and I know you're gonna hate me for it, but we can't have the same Murray we used to have on the show. Who appreciates a good joke more than anybody? *Me.* But who jokes too much? *(Suddenly louder)* You!

MURRAY: Leo, couldn't we talk about this tonight when we get together . . .

LEO'S VOICE *(Softly again)*: It hurt me, Murr', it hurt me what you used to do. When all those thousands of kids wrote in asking for the definition of a chipmunk and you sent back that form letter sayin' a chipmuck was a . . . was a what?

MURRAY: A cute rat.

LEO'S VOICE *(Still soft)*: A cute rat; yeah. I remember my skin broke out somethin' terrible. Some jester you are, foolin' around at the script conferences, foolin' around at the studio. Now, we're not gonna have any more of that, are we?

MURRAY *(Subservient, apologetic)*: No, we won't, I'm sorry, Leo.

LEO'S VOICE: Because we can't fool with the innocence of children, can we? My God, they believe in the little Chipmunk, don't ask me why; I'm nothing; God, I know that. I've been damned lucky. A person like me should get a grand and a half a week for doin' nothin'. I mean, I'm one of the big no-talents of all time, right?

MURRAY: Right . . . I mean, no, Leo, no.

LEO'S VOICE: Oh, I know it's the truth and I don't kid myself about it. But there'll be no more jokin'; right, Murr'? Because I'll tell you the truth, I can't stand it.

MURRAY: Right, Leo.

LEO'S VOICE *(Softly)*: Good. Glad we cleared that up. Because my skin breaks out somethin' terrible. *(Up again)* You're the best, Murray, such talent, you know I love ya, don't ya? You old monkey.

MURRAY *(To* ARNOLD*)*: Please, tell him we'll talk further tonight, too much of him all at once . . .

ARNOLD: Say, Leo, suppose we . . .

LEO'S VOICE: Murray, I want you to put some fifteen-minute fairy tales into the show. You've got your Hans Christian Andersens there, your Grimm Brothers, your Goldilocks, your Sleepin' Beauties, your Gingerbread Men, your Foxy-Loxies, your legends, your folk tales . . . do I reach ya, Murr'?

MURRAY *(Quietly)*: Yeah, Leo . . .

LEO'S VOICE: Now, what I want in those scripts is this, Murray, I want you to give 'em five minutes a action, five minutes a poignancy and then five minutes of the moral message; race-relations thing; world-peace thing; understanding-brings-love thing. I don't know. Shake 'em up a little. Controversy. Angry letters from parents. Kid's show with something to say, get some excitement in the industry, wild . . .

MURRAY *(He leans over very close to speaker-phone; whispers into it)*: Hey, Leo, I might show up one day with eleven minutes of poignancy, no action and a twelve-second moral message . . .

ARNOLD: Murray, stop it . . .

MURRAY *(Shouting into the speaker-phone)*: *And then where would we be?*
　(There is a pause. No sound comes from the speaker-phone. Then:)

LEO'S VOICE: See how he mocks me? Well, I guess there's plenty to mock. Plenty mocking. Sometimes I try to take a cold look at what I am. *(Very soft)* Sweaty Leo jumping around in a funny costume trying to make a buck out of being a chipmunk. The Abominable Snowman in a cute suit. But I'll tell you something, Murray . . . sit down for a minute. (MURRAY *is standing;* LEO'S VOICE *is still fairly pleasant.)* Are ya sitting down, Murray? (MURRAY *remains standing;* LEO'S VOICE *is suddenly loud, sharp, commanding.)* Murray, sit down! *(*MUR-RAY *sits down.)* Good. Now I'm gonna tell you a story . . .

MURRAY: *(Softly, painfully)*: Arnold, he's gonna do it again . . . the story . . .

LEO'S VOICE: Murray . . .

MURRAY *(Softly, miserably)*: The story I got tattooed to my skull . . .

LEO'S VOICE: On June the third . . .

MURRAY *(Hunching over in his chair, looking down at the floor)*: Story number twelve . . . the "Laughter of Children" story . . . again . . .

LEO'S VOICE: I will be forty-two years old . . .

MURRAY *(To* ARNOLD; *painfully, pleading)*: Arnie . . .

LEO'S VOICE: And maybe it's the silliest, phoniest, cop-out thing . . .

LEO'S VOICE and MURRAY *(In unison)*. . . . you ever heard, but the Chipmunk, Chuckles, the little guy I pretend to be, is real to me . . .

LEO'S VOICE: . . . as real to me as . . . as this phone in my hand; those children, don't ask me why, God I don't know, but they believe in that little fellah . . . *(MURRAY looks up from the floor now and over at the speaker-phone, which is on the other side of the room; his eyes are fixed on it.)* Look, Murr', I do what I can for the cash-monies; but also, and I say it without embarrassment, I just love kids, the laughter of children, and we can't have you foolin' with that, Murr', can't have you jokin' . . . *(MURRAY stands up, still looking at the speaker-phone.)* because it's this whole, bright, wild sorta child kinda thing . . . *(MURRAY is walking slowly toward the speaker-phone now; ARNOLD, watching MURRAY, starts to rise from his chair.)* it's this very up feeling, it's all young, and you can't joke with it; the laughter of children; those warm waves, that fresh, open, spontaneous laughter, you can feel it on your face . . .

MURRAY *(Picking the speaker-phone up off the desk)*: Like a sunburn . . .

LEO'S VOICE: Like a sunburn . . .

ARNOLD *(Coming toward MURRAY as if to stop him)*: Murray . . . wait . . .

LEO'S VOICE: And it's a pride thing . . . *(MURRAY turns with the speaker-phone held in his hands and drops it into the wastepaper basket next to the desk. He does this calmly. ARNOLD, too late to stop him, stands watching, dumbly paralyzed. LEO, unaware, goes right on talking, his voice somewhat garbled and echoing from the bottom of the wastepaper basket.)* . . . so then how lovely, how enchanting it is, that I should be paid so well for something I love so much . . . *(Pause)* Say, there's this noise . . . there's this . . . I'm getting this crackling noise on my end here . . . What's happened to the phone?

ARNOLD *(Sadly, solemnly; looking down into the basket)*: Leo, you're in a wastepaper basket.

LEO'S VOICE: That you, Murray? . . . There's this crackling noise . . . I can't hear you . . . Hello? . . . What's going on? . . .

ARNOLD: Leo, hold it just a minute, I'll get you.

LEO'S VOICE: There's this funny noise. . . . Where'd everybody go? Where is everybody? . . . Hello, Murray . . . hello . . . come back . . . come back . . .

ARNOLD *(Fishing amongst the papers in basket for the speaker-phone)*: I'll find you, Leo, I'll find you. . . . *(Finally lifts the speaker out of the basket, holds it gently, tenderly in his hands like a child, speaks soothingly to it.)* Look, Leo . . . Leo, we had a little . . . some trouble with the phone, we . . . *(Realizes that he is getting no reaction from the box.)* Leo? . . . Leo? . . . *(As though the box were a friend whom he thinks might have died, shaking the box tenderly to revive it)* Leo . . . Leo, are you there? . . . Are you there? . . . It's dead. *(Turning to look at MURRAY, as though announcing the demise of a dear one.)* He's gone.

MURRAY: Well, don't look at me like that, Arnie; I didn't *kill* him. He doesn't *live* in that box . . . Or maybe he does.

ARNOLD: A man has a job for you so you drop him in a basket.

MURRAY: Arnie, I quit that nonsense five months ago . . .

ARNOLD: Murray, you're a *nut,* a man has a job for you, there's a hearing on Thursday . . .

MURRAY: A fool in a box telling me what's funny, a Welfare Board checking my underwear every week because I don't look good in their files . . . and *I'm* the nut, right? *I'm* the crazy one.

ARNOLD: Murray, you float like a balloon and everybody's waitin' for ya with a pin. I'm trying to put you in *touch,* Murray . . . with *real things;* with . . .

MURRAY *(Angrily, taking in the office with a sweep of his hand)*: You mean like this office, *real* things, like this office? The world could come to an end and you'd find out about it on the phone. *(Pointing at two framed photographs on* AR-NOLD's *desk)* Pictures of your wife six years ago when she was still a piece, and your kids at their cutest four years ago when they looked best for the office . . . Oh, you're in *touch* all right, Arnie.

ARNOLD *(Softly, soothing)*: Murray, you're just a little excited, that's all, just relax, everything's gonna be fine . . .

MURRAY *(Shouting)*: Damn it . . . get angry; I just insulted you, personally, about your wife, your kids; I just said lousy things to you. Raise your voice, at least your eyebrows . . . *(Pleading painfully)* Please, have an argument with me . . .

ARNOLD *(Coaxing)*: We'll call Leo back, we'll apologize to him . . . *(*MURRAY *goes to the end table, picks up an apple from the bowl of fruit.)* Everything's gonna be just fine, Murray, you'll see . . . just fine.

MURRAY: Arnie?

ARNOLD: Huh?

MURRAY: Catch. *(Tosses the apple underhand across the room.* ARNOLD *catches it.* MURRAY *exits.)*

ARNOLD *(His hand out from catching the apple)*: Aw, Murray . . . *(Lowers his hand to his side; speaks quietly, alone now in the office.)* Murray, I swear to you, King Kong is *not* on top of the Time-Life Building . . .

> *(*ARNOLD *discovers the apple in his hand; bites into it. The lights fade quickly. As they dim, we hear* NICK *humming and whistling "Yes, Sir, That's My Baby." The lights go up on* MURRAY's *apartment.* NICK's *humming and whistling fades back so that it is coming from outside the window; the humming grows louder again after a second or two as, it would seem, he descends the fire-escape ladder from Mrs. Myers' apartment. It is early evening. No one is onstage. The apartment has been rather spectacularly rehabilitated by* SANDRA *since we saw it last. The great clutter of* MURRAY's *nonsense collection, clocks, radios, knickknacks, has been cleared away, the books have been neatly arranged in the bookcases, a hat rack has been placed above the bureau and* MURRAY's *hats are placed neatly on it. There are bright new bedspreads and brightly coloured throw pillows, one new curtain is already up at the windows and a piece of matching material is over the Morris chair. The beach chair and swivel chair are gone and the wicker chair has been painted gold, the table has a bright new cloth over it. Pots of flowers are on the table, the bookshelves, the file cabinets, headboard and desk; and geraniums are in a holder hanging from the window molding. The whole place has been dusted and polished and gives off a bright glow. After two lines or so of the song,* NICK *enters through the window from the fire escape, carrying his pajamas and school books.* NICK *sees the new curtain first, and then, from his position on the window seat, sees the other changes in the apartment and smiles appreciatively.* SANDRA *enters from the kitchen, carrying a mixing bowl and a spoon. She smiles, glad to see* NICK.)*

SANDRA: Hello, Nick . . .

NICK: Hello, lady. I came in from the fire escape. Mrs. Myers lives right upstairs. I went there after school, I . . . *(Indicating her work on the apartment)* Did . . . did you do all this?

SANDRA: Yes, Nick; do you like it?

NICK *(Goes to her, smiling)*: I think it's superb. I mean, imagine my surprise when I saw it. *(Pause)* Where's Murray?

SANDRA *(Happily telling him the good news)*: Nick . . . Murray went downtown to see your Uncle Arnold. He's going to get a job.

NICK: That's terrific. Hey, that's just terrific. *(SANDRA goes to the folded new curtains on the bed, sits down on the bed, unfolds one of the curtains, begins attaching curtain hooks and rings to it; NICK sits next to her, helping her as they talk together.)* See, lady, he was developing into a bum. You don't want to see somebody you like developing into a bum, and doing nutty things, right? You know what he does? He hollers. Like we were on Park Avenue last Sunday, it's early in the morning and nobody is in the street, see, there's just all those big quiet apartment houses; and he hollers "Rich people, I want to see you all out on the street for volley ball! Let's snap it up!" And sometimes, if we're in a crowded elevator some place, he turns to me and yells "Max, there'll be no *more* of this self-pity! You're forty, it's time you got *used* to being a midget!" And everybody stares. And he has a wonderful time. What do you do with somebody who hollers like that? Last week in Macy's he did that. *(He laughs.)* If you want to know the truth, it was pretty funny. *(SANDRA smiles.)* I think you're a very nice lady.

SANDRA: Thank you, Nick.

NICK: What do you think of me?

SANDRA: I think you're very nice also.

NICK: A very nice quality you have is that you are a good listener, which is important to me because of how much I talk. *(She laughs, enjoying him.)* Hey, you're some laugher, aren't you, lady?

SANDRA: I guess so, Nick.

NICK *(Trying to make her feel at home)*: Would you like some fruit? An orange maybe?

SANDRA: No thank you, Nick.

NICK: If you want to call your mother or something, I mean, feel free to use the telephone . . . or my desk if you want to read a book or something . . . or *any* of the chairs . . .

SANDRA: I will, Nick, thank you.

NICK: O.K. *(Pause)* Are you going to be staying around here for a while?

SANDRA: I might, yes.

NICK *(He rises, picks up the pajamas and books he brought in with him; indicates apartment)*: Has . . . has Murray seen . . . all this?

SANDRA: No, not yet.

NICK *(Nods)*: Not yet. Well . . . *(Goes to the window, steps up on window seat.)* Good luck, lady. *(He exits through the window, carrying his pajamas and school books, goes back up the fire escape. SANDRA crosses to window seat, smiling to herself. MURRAY enters, unnoticed by her.)*

MURRAY *(Standing still at the front door, glancing around at the apartment; to himself)*. Oh God, I've been attacked by the *Ladies' Home Journal.*

(SANDRA hears him, goes to him happily.)

SANDRA: Murray, what a nice suit you bought. How is everything, which job did . . .

MURRAY *(Looking around at her work on the apartment)*: Hey look at this. You've started to get rid of the Edgar Allan Poe atmosphere.

SANDRA: Don't you like it?

MURRAY *(Looking around, noticing his knicknacks are missing)*: Sure. Sure. Lotta work. Place has an unusual quality now. Kind of Fun Gothic.

SANDRA: Well, of course I'm really not done yet, the curtains aren't all up, and this chair won't look so bad if we reupholster . . . Come on, Murray, don't keep me in suspense, which one of the jobs did you . . .

MURRAY *(Takes her arm, smiles, seats her on the chair in front of him)*: I shall now leave you breathless with the strange and wondrous tale of this sturdy lad's adventures today in downtown Oz. *(She is cheered by his manner and ready to listen.)* Picture, if you will, me. I am walking on East Fifty-first Street an hour ago and I decided to construct and develop a really decorative, general-all-purpose apology. Not complicated, just the words "I am sorry," said with a little style.

SANDRA: Sorry for what?

MURRAY: Anything. For being late, early, stupid, asleep, silly, alive . . . *(He moves about now, acting out the scene on the street for her.)* Well, y'know when you're walking down the street talking to yourself how sometimes you suddenly say a coupla words out loud? So I said, "I'm sorry," and this fella, complete stranger, he looks up a second and says, "That's all right, Mac," and goes right on. *(MURRAY and SANDRA laugh.)* He automatically forgave me. I communicated. Five-o'clock rush-hour in midtown you say, "Sir, I believe your hair is on fire," and they wouldn't hear you. So I decided to test the whole thing out scientifically, I stayed right there on the corner of Fifty-first and Lex for a while, just saying "I'm sorry" to everybody that went by. *(Abjectly)* "Oh, I'm so sorry, sir . . ." *(Slowly, quaveringly)* "I'm terribly sorry, madam . . . " *(Warmly)* "Say there, miss, I'm sorry." Of course, some people just gave me a funny look, but Sandy, I swear, seventy-five percent of them *forgave* me. *(Acting out the people for her)* "Forget it, buddy" . . . "That's O.K., really." Two ladies forgave me in unison, one fella forgave me from a passing car, and one guy forgave me for his dog. "Poofer forgives the nice man, don't you, Poofer?" Oh, Sandy, it was fabulous. I had tapped some vast reservoir. Something had happened to all of them for which they felt *some*body should apologize. If you went up to people on the street and offered them money, they'd refuse it. But everybody accepts apology immediately. It is the most negotiable currency. I said to them, "I am sorry." And they were all so generous, so kind. You could give 'em love and it wouldn't be accepted half as graciously, as unquestioningly . . .

SANDRA *(Suspiciously, her amusement fading)*: That's certainly . . . that's very interesting, Murray.

MURRAY: Sandy, I could run up on the roof right now and holler, "I am sorry," and half a million people would holler right back, "That's O.K., just see that you don't do it again!"

SANDRA *(After a pause)*: Murray, you didn't take any of the jobs.

MURRAY *(Quietly)*: Sandy, I took whatever I am and put a suit on it and gave it a haircut and took it outside and that's what happened. I know what I said this morning, what I promised, and Sandra, I'm sorry, I'm very sorry. *(She just sits there before him and stares at him expressionlessly.)* Damn it, lady, that was a beautiful apology. You gotta love a guy who can apologize so nice. I rehearsed for over an hour. *(She just looks at him.)* That's the most you should expect from life, Sandy, a really good apology for all the things you won't get.

SANDRA: Murray, I don't understand. What happens to Nick? What about the Welfare Board?

MURRAY *(He takes her hand)*: Sandra . . .

SANDRA: I mean, if you don't like the jobs your brother found for you, then take *any* job . . .

MURRAY *(He takes both of her hands and kneels next to her chair)*: Oh, Sandy . . . *(Softly, pleading for her to understand)* Nick, he's a wonderful kid, but he's brought the God-damned world in on me. Don't you understand, Sandy, they'd be checking up on me every week; being judged by people I don't know and who don't know me, a committee of ghosts; gimme a month of that and I'd turn into an ashtray, a bowl of corn flakes; I wouldn't know me on the street. . . . *(Looks under chair.)* Have you seen Murray? He was here just a minute ago. . . . *(Looks at her, smiles.)* Hey, have you seen Murray? *(Pleading for her to understand)* I wouldn't be of any use to Nick or you or anybody . . .

  (SANDRA moves away from him, goes to the window seat, leaves him kneeling at the chair. She is still holding the curtain she had been working on.)

SANDRA *(Quietly)*: I've had no effect on you at all. I've made no difference. You have no idea what it feels like to have no effect on people. I am not a leader. I scored very low in leadership in three different vocational aptitude tests. When I point my finger, people go the other way . . . *(Absently, she begins to fold the curtain neatly in her lap.)*

MURRAY: Sandra . . .

SANDRA: In grad school they put me in charge of the Structured-Childs-Play-Analysis session one day . . . *(She shrugs.)* and all the children fell asleep. I am not a leader.

MURRAY *(Going to her at the window seat; warmly, with love)*: Oh, Sandy, you are a cute, jolly lady . . . please understand.

SANDRA: When you left this morning, I was so sure . . .

MURRAY: This morning . . . *(He sits next to her on the window seat, his arm around her, his free hand gesturing expansively, romantically.)* Oh, Sandy, I saw the most beautiful sailing this morning . . . The *Sklardahl,* Swedish liner, bound for Europe. It's a great thing to do when you're about to start something new; you see a boat off. It's always wonderful; there's a sailing practically every day this time of year. Sandy, you go down and stand at the dock with all the well-wishers and throw confetti and make a racket with them. . . . Hey, bon voyage, Charley, have a wonderful time. . . . It gives you a genuine feeling of the beginning of things. . . . There's another one Friday, big French ship, two stacker . . .

  (SANDRA has been watching him coldly during this speech; she speaks quietly; catching him in mid-air.)

SANDRA: Nick will have to go away now, Murray. *(She looks away from him.)* I bought new bedspreads at Altman's, I haven't spoken to my mother in two days, and you went to see a boat off. *(She pauses; then smiles to herself for a moment.)* My goodness; I'm a listmaker. *(She leaves him alone in the window seat.)* I have to have enough sense to leave you, Murray. I can see why Nick liked it here. I would like it here too if I was twelve years old. *(She puts the folded curtain down on the chair, picks up her jacket.)*

MURRAY *(Coming toward her, warmly)*: Come on, stick with me, Dr. Markowitz, anything can happen above an abandoned Chinese restaurant. . . .

SANDRA *(Looking directly at him; quietly)*: Maybe you're wonderfully independent, Murray, or maybe, maybe you're the most extraordinarily selfish person I've ever met. *(She picks up her hand bag and starts toward the door.)*

MURRAY *(Tired of begging; angrily, as she walks toward the door)*: What're you gonna do now, go back and live in a closet? It's really gonna be quite thrilling, you and Albert, guarding the Lincoln Tunnel together.

SANDRA *(Turning at the door to look at him)*: I think, Murray, that you live in a much, much larger closet than I do.

MURRAY *(Painfully)*: Lady, lady, please don't look at me like that . . .

SANDRA *(Looking about the apartment; very quietly)*: Oh, there are so many really attractive things you can do with a one-room apartment if you're willing to use your imagination. *(Opens the door.)* Good-bye, Murray. *(She exits. MURRAY stands still for a moment; then rushes forward to the closed door, angrily.)*

MURRAY *(Shouting)*: Hey, damn it, you forgot your files! *(Picks up her files from the bureau, opens the door; but she is gone.)* The management is not responsible for personal property! *(Closes the door, puts the files back on the bureau; stands at the door, looking around at the apartment.)* And what the hell did you do to my apartment? Where are my clocks? What'd you do with my stuff? Where's my radios? *(His back to the audience, shouting)* What've we got here; God damn Sunnybrook Farm! What happened to my place? *(Suddenly realizing he is still wearing a new suit, he pulls off his suit jacket, rolls it up into a tight ball, and throws it violently across the room. A moment; then he relaxes, walks casually to the window, puts his favourite hat on, sits, leans back comfortably in the window seat and smiles. He talks out of the window in a loud mock-serious voice.)* Campers . . . the entertainment committee was quite disappointed by the really poor turn-out at this morning's community sing. I mean, where's all that old Camp Chickawattamee spirit? Now, I'd like to say that I . . . *(He hesitates; he can't think of anything to say. A pause; then he haltingly tries again.)* I'd like to say right now that I . . . that . . . that I . . . *(His voice is soft, vague; he pulls his knees up, folds his arms around them, his head bent on his knees; quietly)* Campers, I can't think of anything to say . . .

　　(A moment; then)

Curtain

ACT THREE

In the darkness, before the curtain goes up, we hear an old recording of a marching band playing "Stars and Stripes Forever." This goes on rather loudly for a few moments. The music diminishes somewhat as the curtain goes up; and we see that the music is coming from an old phonograph on the wicker chair near the bed. It's about thirty minutes later and, though much of SANDRA's work on the apartment is still apparent, it is obvious that MURRAY has been busy putting his place back into its old shape. The curtains are gone, as is the tablecloth and the material on the Morris chair. All the flower pots have been put on top of the file cabinet. The swivel chair and the beach chair are back in view. Cluttered about the room again is much of MURRAY's nonsense collection, clocks, radios, knickknacks and stacks of magazines.

As the curtain goes up, MURRAY has just retrieved a stack of magazines, the megaphone and the pirate pistol from the closet where SANDRA had put them; and we see him now placing them back around the room carefully, as though they were part of some strict design. ARNOLD enters, carrying his attaché case; walks to the beach chair, sits, takes his hat off. The two men do not look at each other. The music continues to play.

ARNOLD *(After a moment)*: I didn't even bring a tangerine with me. That's very courageous if you think about it for a minute. *(Looks over at MURRAY, who is not facing him, points at record player.)* You wanna turn that music off, please? *(No reply from MURRAY.)* Murray, the music; I'm trying to . . . *(No reply from MURRAY, so ARNOLD puts his attaché case and hat on table, goes quickly to the record player and turns the music off; MURRAY turns to look at ARNOLD.)* O.K., I'm a little slow. It takes me an hour to get insulted. Now I'm insulted. You walked out of my office. That wasn't a nice thing to do to me, Murray . . . *(MURRAY does not reply.)* You came into my office like George God; everybody's supposed to come up and audition for Human Being in front of you. *(Comes over closer to him, takes his arm.)* Aw, Murray, today, one day, leave the dragons alone, will ya? And look at the dragons you pick on; Sloan, Leo, me; silly old arthritic dragons, step on a toe and we'll start to cry. Murray, I called Leo back, I apologized, told him my phone broke down; I got him to come over here tonight. He's anxious to see you, everything's O.K. . . . .

MURRAY: Hey, you just never give up, do you, Arnie?

ARNOLD: Listen to me, Murray, do I ever tell you what to do . . .

MURRAY: Yes, all the time.

ARNOLD: If you love this kid, then you gotta take any kinda stupid job to keep him . . .

MURRAY: Now you're an expert on love.

ARNOLD: Not an expert, but I sure as hell value my amateur standing. Murray, about him leaving, have you told him yet?

MURRAY *(Softly; realizing ARNOLD's genuine concern)*: Arnie, don't worry, I know how to handle it. I've got a coupla days to tell him. And don't underrate Nick, he's gonna understand this a lot better than you think.

ARNOLD: Murray, I finally figured out your problem. There's only one thing that really bothers you . . . *(With a sweep of his hand)* Other people. *(With a mock-secretive tone)* If it wasn't for them other people, everything would be great, huh, Murray? I mean, you think everything's fine, and then you go out into the street . . . and there they all *are* again, right? The Other People; taking up space, bumping into you, asking for things, making lines to wait on, taking cabs away from ya . . . The Enemy . . . Well, *watch* out, Murray, they're everywhere . . .

MURRAY: Go ahead, Arnie, give me advice. At thirty thousand a year you can afford it.

ARNOLD: Oh, I get it, if I'm so smart why ain't I poor? You better get a damn good act of your own before you start giving *mine* the razzberry. What's this game you play gonna be like ten years from now, without youth? Murray, Murray, I can't *watch* this, you gotta *shape* up . . .

MURRAY *(Turning quickly to face* ARNOLD; *in a surprised tone)*: Shape *up*? *(Looks directly at* ARNOLD: *speaks slowly.)* Arnie, what the hell happened to you? You got so old. I don't know you any more. When you quit "Harry the Fur King" on Thirty-eighth Street, remember?

ARNOLD: That's twenty years ago, Murray.

MURRAY: You told me you were going to be in twenty businesses in twenty years if you had to, till you found out what you wanted. Things were always going to change. Harry said you were not behaving maturely enough for a salesman; your clothes didn't match or something . . . *(Laughs in affectionate memory of the event.)* So the next day, you dressed perfectly, homburg, gray suit, cuff links, carrying a briefcase and a rolled umbrella . . . and you came into Harry's office on roller skates. You weren't going to take crap from *any*body. So that's the business you finally picked . . . taking crap from *every*body.

ARNOLD: I don't do practical jokes any more, if that's what you mean . . .

MURRAY *(Grabs both of* ARNOLD's *arms tensely)*: Practical, that's right; a way to stay alive. If most things aren't funny, Arn, then they're only exactly what they are; then it's one long dental appointment interrupted occasionally by something exciting, like waiting or falling asleep. What's the point if I leave everything exactly the way I find it? Then I'm just adding to the noise, then I'm just taking up some more room on the subway.

ARNOLD: Murray, the Welfare Board has these specifications; all you have to do is meet a couple specifications . . .

*(*MURRAY *releases his grip on* ARNOLD's *arms;* MURRAY's *hands drop to his sides.)*

MURRAY: Oh, Arnie, you don't understand any more. You got that wide stare that people stick in their eyes so nobody'll know their head's asleep. You got to be a shuffler, a moaner. You want me to come sit and eat fruit with you and watch the clock run out. You start to drag and stumble with the rotten weight of all the people who should have been told off, all the things you should have said, all the specifications that aren't yours. The only thing you got left to reject is your food in a restaurant if they do it wrong and you can send it back and make a big fuss with the waiter . . . *(*MURRAY *turns away from* ARNOLD, *goes to the window seat, sits down.)* Arnold, five months ago I forgot what *day* it was. I'm on the subway on my way to work and I didn't know what day it was and it scared the hell out of me . . . . *(Quietly)* I was sitting in the express looking out the window same as every morning watching the local stops go by in the dark with an empty head and my arms folded, not feeling great and not feeling rotten, just not feeling, and for a minute I couldn't remember, I didn't know, unless I really concentrated, whether it was a Tuesday or a Thursday . . . or a . . . for a minute it could have been *any* day, Arnie . . . sitting in the train going through any day . . . in the dark through any year . . . . Arnie, it scared the hell out of me. *(Stands up.)* You got to know what day it is. You got to know what's the name of the game and what the rules are with nobody else telling you. You have to own your days and name them, each one of them, every one of them, or else the years go right by and none of them belong to you. *(Turns to look at* ARNOLD.*)* And that ain't just for weekends, kiddo . . . *(Looks at* ARNOLD *a moment longer, then speaks in a pleasant tone.)* Here it is, the day after Irving R. Feldman's birthday, for God's sake . . . *(Takes a hat, puts it on.)* And I never even congratulated him . . . *(Starts to walk briskly toward the front door.* ARNOLD *shouts in a voice stronger than we have ever heard from him.)*

ARNOLD: Murray! *(*MURRAY *stops, turns, startled to hear this loud a voice from* ARNOLD. ARNOLD *looks fiercely at* MURRAY *for a moment, then* ARNOLD *looks surprised, starts to laugh.)*

MURRAY: What's so funny?

ARNOLD: Wow, I scared myself. You hear that voice? Look at that, I got you to stop, I got your complete, full attention, the floor is mine now . . . *(Chuckles awkwardly.)* And I can't think of a God-damned thing to say . . . *(Shrugs his shoulders; picks up his hat from the table.)* I have long been aware, Murray . . . I have long been aware that you don't respect me much. . . . I suppose there are a lot of brothers who don't get along. . . . But in reference . . . to us, considering the factors . . . *(Smiles, embarrassed.)* Sounds like a contract, doesn't it? *(Picks up his briefcase, comes over to* MURRAY.*)* Unfortunately for you, Murray, you want to be a hero. Maybe, if a fella falls into a lake, you can jump in and save him; there's still that kind of stuff. But who gets opportunities like that in midtown Manhattan, with all that traffic. *(Puts on his hat.)* I am willing to deal with the available world and I do not choose to shake it up but to live with it. There's the people who spill things, and the people who get spilled on; I do not choose to notice the stains, Murray. I have a wife and I have children, and business, like they say, is business. I am not an exceptional man, so it is possible for me to stay with things the way they are. I'm lucky. I'm gifted. I have a talent for surrender. I'm at peace. But you are cursed; and I like you so it makes me sad, you don't have the gift; and I see the torture of it. All I can do is worry for you. But I will not worry for myself; you cannot convince me that I am one of the Bad Guys. I get up, I go, I lie a little, I peddle a little, I watch the rules, I talk the talk. We fellas have those offices high up there so we can catch the wind and go with it, however it blows. But, and I will not apologize for it, I take pride; I am the best possible Arnold Burns. *(Pause)* Well . . . give my regards to Irving R. Feldman, will ya? *(He starts to leave.)*

MURRAY *(Going toward him)*: Arnold . . .

ARNOLD: Please, Murray . . . *(Puts his hand up.)* Allow me once to leave a room before you do.

> *(*ARNOLD *snaps on record player as he walks past it to the front door; he exits.* MURRAY *goes toward the closed door, the record player has warmed up and we suddenly hear "Stars and Stripes Forever" blaring loudly from the machine again;* MURRAY *turns at this sound and stands for a long moment looking at the record player as the music comes from it.* NICK *enters through the window from the fire escape, unnoticed by* MURRAY. NICK *looks about, sees that the apartment is not quite what it was an hour before.)*

NICK: Hey, Murray . . .

MURRAY *(Turns, sees* NICK*)*: Nick . . . *(Turns the record player off; puts the record on the bed.)*

NICK: Hey, where's the lady?

MURRAY: Well, she's not here right now . . .

NICK *(Stepping forward to make an announcement)*: Murray, I have decided that since *you* are getting a job today then I made up my mind it is time for *me* also to finish a certain matter which I have been putting off.

MURRAY: Nick, listen, turned out the only job I could get in a hurry was with Chuckles . . .

NICK *(Nodding in approval)*: Chuckles, huh? Well, fine. *(Then, grimly)* Just as long as I don't have to watch that terrible program every morning. *(Returning to his announcement)* For many months now I have been concerned with a decision, Murray . . . Murray, you're not listening.

MURRAY *(Distracted)*: Sure I'm listening, yeah . . .

NICK: The past couple months I have been thinking about different names and considering different names because in four weeks I'm gonna be thirteen and I gotta pick my permanent name, like we said.

MURRAY: Why don't you just go on calling yourself Nick? You've been using it the longest.

NICK: Nick is a name for a short person. And since I am a short person I do not believe I should put a lot of attention on it.

MURRAY: Whaddya mean, where'd you get the idea you were short?

NICK: From people who are taller than I am.

MURRAY: That's ridiculous.

NICK: Sure, standing up there it's ridiculous, but from down here where I am it's not so ridiculous. And half the girls in my class are taller than me. Especially Susan Bookwalter. (NICK *sits dejectedly in the swivel chair.)*

MURRAY *(Crouching over next to him)*: Nick, you happen to be a nice medium height for your age.

NICK *(Pointing at* MURRAY*)*: Yeah, so how is it everybody crouches over a little when I'm around?

MURRAY *(Straightening up)*: Because you're a kid. *(Sits next to him.)* Listen, you come from a fairly tall family. Next couple years you're gonna grow like crazy. Really, Nick, every day you're getting bigger.

NICK: So is Susan Bookwalter. *(Stands.)* So for a couple of months I considered various tall names. Last month I considered, for a while, Zachery, but I figured there was a chance Zachery could turn into a short, fat, bald name. Then I thought about Richard, which is not really tall, just very thin with glasses. Then last week I finally, really, decided and I took out a new library card to see how it looks and today I figured I would make it definite and official. *(He takes a library card out of his pocket, hands it to* MURRAY.*)*

MURRAY *(Looks at the card, confused)*: This is *my* library card.

NICK: No, that's the whole thing; it's mine.

MURRAY: But it says "*Murray* Burns" on it . . .

NICK: Right, that's the name I picked. So I took out a new card to see how it looks and make it official.

MURRAY *(Looks at the card, is moved and upset by it, but covers with cool dignity; stands, speaks very formally)*: Well, Nick, I'm flattered . . . I want you to know that I'm . . . very flattered by this. (NICK *goes to the alcove to put his school books and pajamas away.)* Well, why the hell did you . . . I mean, damn it, Nick, that's too many Murrays, very confusing . . . *(MURRAY begins to shift the card awkwardly from one hand to the other, speaks haltingly.)* Look, why don't you call yourself George, huh? Very strong name there, George . . .

NICK *(Shaking his head firmly)*: No. We made a deal it was up to me to pick which name and that's the name I decided on; "Murray."

MURRAY: Well, what about Jack? What the hell's wrong with Jack? Jack Burns . . . sounds like a promising heavyweight.

NICK: I like the name I picked better.

MURRAY *(Very quietly)*: Or Martin . . . or Robert . . .

NICK: Those names are all square.

LEO's VOICE *(From behind the door, shouting)*: Is this it? Is this the Lion's Den, here? Hey, Murr'!

MURRAY *(Softly)*: Ah, I heard the voice of a chipmunk.

NICK *(Going into the bathroom)*: I better go put on a tie.

MURRAY *(Goes to the door; stands there a moment, looks over to the other side of the room at NICK, who is offstage in the bathroom; smiles, speaks half to himself, very softly)*. You coulda called yourself Charlie. Charlie is a very musical name.

> *(Then, he opens the door. LEO HERMAN enters. He wears a camel's-hair coat and hat. The coat, like his suit, is a little too big for him. He is carrying a paper bag and a large Chuckles statue—a life-size cardboard cutout of himself in his character of Chuckles the Chipmunk; the statue wears a blindingly ingratiating smile.)*

LEO *(With great enthusiasm)*: Murray, there he is! There's the old monkey! There's the old joker, right?

MURRAY *(Quietly, smiling politely)*: Yeah, Leo, here he is. *(Shakes LEO's hand.)* It's . . . it's very nice to see you again, Leo, after all this time.

LEO *(Turning to see NICK, who has come out of the bathroom wearing his tie)*: There he is! There's the little guy! *(Goes to NICK carrying the statue and the paper bag.)* Looka here, little guy . . . *(Setting the statue up against the wall next to the window.)* I gotta Chuckles statue for you.

NICK *(With his best company manners)*: Thank you, Mr. Herman; imagine how pleased I am to receive it. It's a very artistic statue and very good cardboard too.

LEO *(Taking a Chuckles hat from the paper bag; a replica of the furry, big-eared hat worn by the statue)*: And I gotta Chuckles hat for you too, just like the old Chipmunk wears. *(He puts the hat on NICK's head.)*

NICK: Thank you.

LEO *(Crouching over to NICK's height)*: Now that you've got the Chuckles hat, you've got to say the Chuckles-hello.

NICK *(Confused, but anxious to please)*: The what?

LEO *(Prompting him)*: "Chip-chip, Chippermunkie!" *(He salutes.)*

NICK: Oh, yeah . . . "Chip-chip, Chippermunkie!" *(He salutes too.)*

LEO: May I know your name?

NICK: It's Nick, most of the time.

LEO: Most of the . . . *(Pulling two bags of potato chips from his overcoat pockets)* Say, look what I've got, two big bags of Chuckle-Chip potato chips! How'd ya like to put these crispy chips in some bowls or somethin' for us, huh? *(NICK takes the two bags, goes to the kitchen.)* And take your time, Nick, your uncle 'n' me have some grown-up talkin' to do. *(After* NICK *exits into the kitchen)* The kid hates me. I can tell. Didn't go over very well with him, pushed a little too hard. He's a nice kid, Murray.

MURRAY: How are *your* kids, Leo?

LEO: Fine, fine. But, Murray, I swear, even *they* don't like my show since you stopped writing it. My youngest one . . . my six-year-old . . . *(He can't quite remember.)*

MURRAY: Ralphie.

LEO: Ralphie; he's been watching the Funny Bunny Show now every morning instead of me. *(Begins pacing up and down.)* Oh *boy,* have I been bombing out on the show. Murray, do you know what it *feels* like to bomb out in front of children? You flop out in front of kids and, Murray, I swear to God, they're ready to *kill* you. *(Stops pacing.)* Or else, they just stare at you, that's the worst, that hurt, innocent stare like you just killed their pup or raped their turtle or something. *(Goes over to* MURRAY.*)* Murray, to have you back with me on the show, to see you at the studio again tomorrow, it's gonna be *beautiful.* You're the *best.*

MURRAY: I appreciate your feeling that way, Leo.

LEO: This afternoon, Murray, on the phone, you hung up on me, didn't you?

MURRAY: I'm sorry Leo, I was just kidding . . . I hope you . . .

LEO *(Sadly)*: Murray, why do you do that to me? Aw, don't tell me, I know, I make people nervous. Who can listen to me for ten minutes? *(Begins pacing up and down again, strokes his tie.)* See *that?* See how I keep touching my suit and my tie? I keep touching myself to make sure I'm still there. Murray, I get this feeling, maybe I vanished when I wasn't looking.

MURRAY: Oh, I'm sure that you're here, Leo.

LEO *(Pointing at* MURRAY*)*: See how he talks to me? A little nasty. *(Smiles suddenly.)* Well, I like it. It's straight and it's real and I like it. You know what I got around me on the show? Finks, dwarfs, phonies and frogs. No Murrays. The show: boring, boredom, bore . . . *(Cups his hands around his mouth and shouts.)* boring, boring . . .

> *(During these last few words,* SANDRA *has entered through the partly open door.* MURRAY *turns, sees her.)*

SANDRA *(Staying near the doorway; reserved, official)*: Murray, I believe that I left my files here; I came to get my files; may I have my files, please. I . . . *(She sees* LEO, *comes a few feet into the room.)* Oh, excuse me . . .

MURRAY *(Cordially, introducing them)*: Chuckles the Chipmunk . . . this is Minnie Mouse.

LEO *(Absently)*: Hi, Minnie . . .

SANDRA *(Looking from one to the other taking in the situation, smiles; to* LEO*)*: You must be . . . you must be Mr. Herman.

LEO *(Mumbling to himself)*: Yeah, I must be. I must be him; I'd rather not be, but what the hell . . .

SANDRA *(Smiling, as she turns right around and goes to the door)*: Well, I'll be on my way . . . *(She exits.* MURRAY *picks up her files from the bureau, goes to the door with them.)*

LEO *(Interrupting* MURRAY *on his way to the door)*: Very attractive girl, that Minnie; what does she do?

MURRAY: She's my decorator.

LEO *(Looking around the apartment)*: Well, she's done a *wonderful* job! *(Indicating the apartment with a sweep of his hand.)* This place is great. It's loose, it's open, it's free. Love it. Wonderful, crazy place. My God . . . you must make out like mad in this place, huh? *(MURRAY closes the door, puts the files back on the bureau; LEO is walking around the apartment.)* How come I never came here before?

MURRAY: You were here last January, Leo.

LEO: Funny thing, work with me for three years and I never saw your apartment.

MURRAY: You were here last January, Leo.

LEO *(Stops pacing, turns to MURRAY)*: Wait a minute, wait a minute, wasn't I here recently, in the winter? Last January, I think . . . *(Goes over to* Murray.*)* Oh, I came here to get you back on the show and you wouldn't listen, you went into the kitchen, sang "Yes Sir, That's My Baby." I left feeling very foolish, like I had footprints on my face . . . You old monkey. *(Smiles, musses up MURRAY's hair.)* You're an old monkey, aren't ya? *(Starts pacing again.)* You know what I got from that experience? A rash. I broke out something terrible. . . . Minnie Mouse! *(Stops pacing.)* Minnie *Mouse! (Laughs loudly, points at the door.)* You told me her name was Minnie Mouse! I swear to God, Murray, I think my mission in life is to feed you straight-lines . . . *(Taking in the apartment with a sweep of his hand.)* It's kind of a fall-out shelter, that's what you got here, Murr', protection against the idiots in the atmosphere. Free, freer, freest . . . *(Cups his hands around his mouth, shouts.)* Free! Free! *(Takes off his coat.)* Another year and I'm gonna cut loose from the God-damn Chipmunk show. Binds me up, hugs me. Finks, dwarfs, phonies and frogs . . . *(Following MURRAY to the window seat)* Two of us should do something new, something wild; new kind of kid's show, for adults maybe . . .

MURRAY *(Sitting on the window seat)*: You told me the same thing three years ago, Leo.

LEO *(Sits next to MURRAY)*: Well, whaddya want from me? I'm a coward; everybody knows that. *(Suddenly seeing the Chuckles statue against the wall next to him.)* Oh God! *(Points at the statue; in anguish)* Did you ever see anything so immodest? I bring a big statue of myself as a gift for a child! I mean, the *pure ego* of it . . . *(Covers his face with his hands.)* I am ashamed. Murray, could you throw a sheet over it or something . . . *(Sees NICK, who has just come out of the kitchen with two bowls of potato chips.)* Mmmm, good! Here they are. (Grabs one bowl from NICK's *hand, gives it to* MURRAY. *Then* LEO *turns to* NICK, *assumes the character and the voice of Chuckles the Chipmunk; a great mock-frown on his face, he goes into a routine for* NICK.*)* Oh, goshes, Kidderoonies, look at your poor Chippermunk friend; he got his mouff stuck. No matter how hard I try I can't get my mouth unstuck. But maybe—if you Chippermunks yell, "Be happy, Chuckles," maybe then it'll get unstuck . . . *(LEO waits. NICK does not react. LEO prompts NICK in a whisper.)* You're supposed to yell, "Be happy, Chuckles."

NICK: Oh yeah . . . sure . . . *(Glances quickly at MURRAY; then, a little embarrassed, he yells.)* Be happy, Chuckles!

LEO: Oh boy! *(His frown changes to a giant smile.)* You *fixed* me! Looka my mouff! *(He jumps up in the air.)* Now I'm all fixed! *(Gets no reaction from NICK. NICK stands patiently in front of LEO.)*

NICK *(Offering the other bowl of potato chips to LEO, trying to be polite)*: Mr. Herman, don't you want your . . .

LEO *(Not accepting the potato chips, speaking in his own voice again, stroking his tie nervously)*: That was a bit from tomorrow morning's show. You'll know it ahead of all the kids in the neighbourhood.

NICK: Thank you.

LEO: That . . . that was one of the funny parts there, when I couldn't move my mouth.

NICK: Yeah?

LEO: Didn't you think it was funny?

NICK: Yeah, that was pretty funny.

LEO *(Smiling nervously)*: Well, don't you laugh or something when you see something funny?

NICK: It just took me by surprise is all. So I didn't get a chance. *(Offering him the potato chips, politely)* Here's your . . .

LEO: Another funny part was when I jumped up with the smile there, at the end there. That was another one.

NICK: Uh-huh.

LEO *(Pressing on, beginning to get tense)*: And the finish on the bit, see, I've got the smile . . . (NICK, *looking trapped, stands there as* LEO *switches back to his Chipmunk voice and puts a giant smile on his face.)* Now I'm aaaall fixed, Chippermunks! *(Suddenly mock-pathos in his eyes.)* Oooops! *Now* I got stuck the *other* way! Oh, *oh,* now my face is stuck the *other* way! *(Throws up his arms, does a loose-legged slapstick fall back onto the floor. Remains prone, waiting for* NICK's *reaction.* NICK *stands there looking at* LEO *quite solemnly.)*

NICK *(Nods his head up and down approvingly)*: That's terrific, Mr. Herman. *(With admiration)* That's all you have to do, you just get up and do that and they pay you and everything.

LEO: You didn't laugh.

NICK: I was waiting for the funny part.

LEO *(Sits up)*: That was the funny part.

NICK: Oh, when you fell down on the . . .

LEO: When I fell down on the floor here.

NICK: See, the thing is, I was . . .

LEO *(Gets up from the floor, paces up and down tensely)*: I know, waiting for the funny part. Well, you missed another funny part.

NICK: Another one. Hey, I'm really sorry, Mr. Herman, I . . .

LEO: Forget it . . . I just happen to know that that bit is very *funny.* I can prove it to you. *(Takes small booklet from pocket, opens it, shows it to* NICK.*)* Now, what does that say there, second line there?

NICK *(Reading from the booklet)*: "Frown bit; eighty-five percent of audience; outright prolonged laughter on frown bit."

LEO: That's the analysis report the agency did for me on Monday's preview audience. The routine I just did for you, got outright prolonged laughter; eighty-five percent.

MURRAY: You could try him on sad parts, Leo; he's very good on sad parts.

LEO *(Goes to* MURRAY *at the window seat, shows him another page in the booklet)*: Matter fact, there's this poignant-type bit I did at the Preview Theatre: "Sixty percent of audience; noticeably moved."

MURRAY: They left the theatre?

LEO *(Tensely, angrily)*: There he is; there's the old joker; Murray the joker, right?

NICK: I do some routines. I can imitate the voice of Alexander Hamilton.

LEO: That's lovely, but I . . .

NICK: I do Alexander Hamilton and Murray does this terrific Thomas Jefferson; we got the voices just right.

MURRAY *(In a dignified voice; to NICK)*: Hello there, Alex, how are you?

NICK *(In a dignified voice; to MURRAY)*: Hello there, Tom; say, you should have been in Congress this morning. My goodness, there was quite a discussion on . . .

LEO: Now, that's *ridiculous.* You . . . you can't *do* an imitation of Alexander Hamilton; nobody knows what he *sounds* like . . .

NICK *(Pointing triumphantly at LEO)*: That's the *funny* part.

MURRAY *(Shaking his head regretfully)*: You missed the funny part, Leo.

LEO *(Walking away from them)*: I'm getting a terrible rash on my neck. *(Turns to them, growing louder and more tense with each word.)* The routine I did for him was *funny.* I was workin' good in front of the kid, I know how to use my God-damn *warmth,* I don't go over with these odd kids; I mean, here I am right in *front* of him, in *person* for God's sake, and he's *staring* at me . . . *(Moves toward them, on the attack.)* It's oddness here, Murray, *odd*ness. Alexander Hamilton imitations! Jaded jokes for old men. Murray, what you've done to this kid. It's a damn shame, a child can't enjoy little animals, a damn shame . . . *(Really on the attack now; waving at the apartment, shouting)* The way you brought this kid up, Murray, grotesque atmosphere, *unhealthy,* and you're not even guilty about it, women in and out, *dec*orators; had he been brought up by a *normal* person and not in this *mad*house . . .

NICK *(Quietly, going toward LEO)*: Hey, don't say that . . .

LEO: A certain kind of freakish way of growing up . . .

NICK *(Quietly)*: Hey, are you calling me a freak? You called me a freak. Take back what you said.

LEO *(Walks away from them, mumbling to himself)*: On June third I will be forty-two years old and I'm standing here arguing with a twelve-year-old kid . . . (LEO *quiets down, turns, comes toward* NICK, *sits on bed,* NICK *standing next to him; speaks calmly to* NICK.) See, Nicky, humour is a cloudy, wonderful thing, but simple and clear like the blue, blue sky. All I want is your simple, honest child's opinion of my routine; for children are too honest to be wise . . .

NICK *(Looking directly at LEO, calmly, quietly, slowly)*: My simple, child's reaction to what you did is that you are not funny. Funnier than you is even Stuart Sloss-man my friend who is eleven and puts walnuts in his mouth and makes noises. What is not funny is to call us names and what is mostly not funny is how sad you are that I would feel sorry for you if it wasn't for how dull you are and those are the worst-tasting potato chips I ever tasted. And that is my opinion from the blue, blue sky.

> (NICK and LEO *stay in their positions, looking at each other. A moment; then* MURRAY *throws his head back and laughs uproariously.* LEO *stands; the bowl of potato chips tips over in his hand, the chips spilling onto the floor.)*

LEO *(Seeing MURRAY's laughter, goes to him at the Morris chair; angrily)*: Murray the joker, right? You didn't want to come back to work for me, you just got me up here to step on my face again! (NICK, *unnoticed by* LEO, *has gone quickly into his alcove and comes out now with his ukulele, playing and singing "Yes, Sir, That's My Baby" with great spirit.* LEO, *hearing this, turns to look at* NICK.) It's the *song. It's the good-bye song. (LEO grabs his hat and coat quickly, as* NICK *goes on playing, starts for front door, shouting.)* Getting *out*, bunch of *nuts* here, *crazy* people . . .

MURRAY: Leo, wait . . . *(Goes to the door to stop* LEO.*)* Leo, wait . . . I'm sorry . . . wait . . . *(LEO stops at the door;* MURRAY *goes down toward* NICK, *who is near the alcove, still playing the song.)* Nick, you better stop now . . .

NICK: Come on, Murray, get your uke, we'll sing to him and he'll go away . . .

MURRAY *(Quietly)*: Nick, we can't . . . *(Gently taking the uke from* NICK, *puts it on the window seat.)* Just put this down, huh?

NICK *(Confused by this; urgently)*: Come on, Murray, let him go away, he called us names, we gotta get rid of him . . .

MURRAY: Quiet now, Nick . . . just be quiet for a minute . . . *(Starts to go back toward* LEO.*)*

NICK *(Shouting)*: Murray, please let him go away . . . *(NICK, seeing the Chuckles statue next to him against the wall, grabs it angrily, throws it down on the floor.)* It's a crummy statue . . . that crummy statue . . . *(Begins to kick the statue fiercely, jumping up and down on it, shouting.)* It's a terrible statue, rotten cardboard . . .

(MURRAY *comes quickly back to* NICK, *holds both of his arms, trying to control him.)*

MURRAY: Aw, Nick, please, no more now, stop it . . .

(There is a great struggle between them; NICK *is fighting wildly to free himself from* MURRAY's *arms.)*

NICK *(Near tears, shouting)*: We don't want jerks like that around here, Murray, let him go away, we gotta get rid of him, Murray, we gotta get rid of him . . .

MURRAY *(Lifts the struggling* NICK *up into his arms, hugging him to stop him.)*: No, Nick . . . I'm sorry, Nick . . . we can't . . . *(NICK gives up, hangs limply in* MURRAY's *arms.* MURRAY *speaks quietly, with love.)* I'm sorry . . . I'm sorry, kid . . . I'm sorry . . . *(He puts* NICK *down, still holding him.)*

NICK *(After a pause; quietly, in disbelief)*: Murray . . .

MURRAY: You better go to your room.

NICK: This is a one-room apartment.

MURRAY: Oh. Then go to your alcove. *(NICK waits a moment, then turns, betrayed, walks over to his alcove, lies down on the bed.* MURRAY *looks over at* LEO, *who is standing at the front door. He walks slowly over to* LEO, *looking down at the floor; humbly)* Leo . . . hope you didn't misunderstand . . . we were just kidding you . . . we . . .

LEO *(Coming toward* MURRAY, *apologetically)*: I, myself, I got carried away there myself.

MURRAY: We all got a little excited, I guess. *(Reaches out to shake* LEO's *hand.)* So, I'll see you at work in the morning, Leo.

LEO *(Smiling, shaking* MURRAY's *hand)*: Great to have you back, fellah. *(Pause)* You both hate me.

MURRAY: Nobody hates you, Leo.

LEO: I hollered at the kid, I'm sorry. I didn't mean to cause any upset. I don't get along too good with kids . . .

MURRAY: Don't worry about it.

LEO: Wanna come have a drink with me, Murray? We could . . .

MURRAY: No thanks; maybe another night, Leo.

LEO: Look, after I leave, you horse around a little with the kid, he'll feel better.

MURRAY: Right, Leo.

LEO *(Pauses; then comes closer to* MURRAY*)*: Murray . . . that bit I did was funny, wasn't it?

MURRAY *(After a moment)*: Yeah, Leo . . . I guess it was just a bad day for you.

LEO *(Pointing at the Chuckles statue on the floor; quietly, but giving a command)*: You don't want to leave that statue lying around like that, huh, Murray?

MURRAY: Oh, no. *(Goes to statue obediently, lifts it up off the floor, leans it upright against the wall.)* There.

LEO: Fine.

MURRAY: See you tomorrow, Leo.

LEO *(Smiles)*: Yeah, see ya tomorrow at the studio . . . *(Ruffles up* MURRAY's *hair.)* You old monkey. *(Goes to the door.)* Hey, you're an old monkey, aren't you?

> *(*LEO *exits.* MURRAY *stays at the door for a moment.* NICK *is sitting on the alcove step, his back to* MURRAY.*)*

MURRAY *(Walking over to* NICK, *trying to make peace with him)*: Say, I could use a roast-turkey sandwich right now, couldn't you, Nick? On rye, with cold slaw and Russian dressing. . . .

> *(*NICK *does not reply.* MURRAY *sits down next to him on the alcove step.* NICK *refuses to look at* MURRAY. *They are both silent for a moment.)*

NICK: Guy calls us names. Guy talks to us like that. Shoulda got rid of that moron. Coulda fooled the Welfare people or something . . . *(*SANDRA *enters through the partly open door, unnoticed by them; she stays up in the doorway, watching them.)* We coulda gone to Mexico or New Jersey or someplace.

MURRAY: I hear the delicatessen in Mexico is terrible.

NICK *(After a moment)*: I'm gonna call myself *Theodore*.

MURRAY: As long as you don't call yourself Beatrice.

NICK: O.K., fool around. Wait'll you see a Theodore running around here. *(Silent for a moment, his back still to* MURRAY; *then, quietly)* Another coupla seconds he would abeen out the door . . . *(Turns to look at* MURRAY.*)* Why'd you go chicken on me, Murray? What'd you stop me for?

MURRAY: Because your routines give me outright prolonged laughter, Theodore.

SANDRA *(After a pause)*: Four ninety-five for this tablecloth and you leave it around like this . . . *(Picks up the discarded tablecloth from the chair.)* A perfectly new tablecloth and already there are stains on it . . . *(Sits on the Morris chair, starts to dab at the tablecloth with her handkerchief.)* You know, it's very interesting that I left my files here. That I forgot them. I mean, psychologically, if you want to analyze that. Of course, last month I left my handbag in the Automat, and I have no idea what that means at all. *(*MURRAY *leaves alcove, starts toward her.)* I think that the pattern of our relationship, if we examine it, is very intricate, the different areas of it, especially the whole "good-bye" area of it, and also the "hello" and "how-are-you" area . . . of it.

MURRAY *(Standing next to her chair now, smiles warmly)*: Hello, Sandy, and how are you?

SANDRA *(Looks up at him, smiles politely)*: Hello, Murray. *(Goes right back to her work, rubbing the tablecloth with her handkerchief.)* You're standing in my light.

MURRAY: Oh. *(He retreats a step.)*

NICK *(Walking over to her)*: Hello, lady.

SANDRA: Hello, Nick.

NICK *(Indicating her work on the tablecloth)*: Lady, can I help you with any of that?

SANDRA: Matter of fact, Nick . . . *(She stands; her arm around* NICK, *she goes to centre with him.)* Nick, I don't think the effect, I mean, the overall design of this room, is really helped by all these . . . *(Gesturing to* MURRAY's *stuff around the bed)* these knickknacks.

NICK: You mean the junk?

SANDRA: Yes.

NICK: Yeah, not too good for the overall design.

SANDRA: If you'd just put them away in that carton there. *(She indicates a carton near the bed.)*

NICK: Sure, lady . . .

(NICK goes quickly to the carton, begins to put MURRAY's *junk into it— some radios, a megaphone, some clocks.* SANDRA *starts putting the tablecloth on the table.)*

MURRAY *(Realizes that they are taking over, moves forward, trying to halt the proceedings)*: Hey, Sandy, now wait a minute . . . *(She goes on with her work, putting a piece of material over the Morris chair. He turns at the sound of one of his radio cabinets being dropped into the carton by* NICK.*)* Listen, Nick, I didn't tell you to . . . Nick . . .

NICK *(Looking up from his work)*: Wilbur . . . *(Drops a clock into the carton.)* Wilbur Malcolm Burns.

(SANDRA is putting the flowers back around the room, picking up the magazines.)

MURRAY *(Protesting)*: Hey, now, both of you, will ya wait a minute here, will ya just wait . . . *(They ignore him, going on with their work. He shrugs, defeated; gives up, goes over to the windows, away from them, sits down sadly in the window seat.)* Wonder what kind of weather we got out there tonight. *(Looks out of window; as usual, he can see nothing but the gray, blank wall of the building a few feet opposite; sadly, to himself)* Never can see the God-damned weather. We got a permanent fixture out there: twilight in February. Some day that damn building'll fall down into Seventh Avenue so I can see the weather. *(Leans over, begins to talk out of the window.)* Everybody onstage for the Hawaiian number, please . . . *(SANDRA, during these last few lines, has gone to the phone, dialed. Listened a few moments and hung up.* MURRAY *hears her hang up, turns to her.)* What're you doing?

SANDRA: I just spoke to the Weather Lady. She says it's a beautiful day. *(She goes back to her work on the apartment.)*

MURRAY *(He continues to talk out the window, softly at first)*: Well, then, if you're not ready, we better work on the Military March number. Now the last time we ran this, let's admit it was pretty ragged. I mean, the whole "Spirit of '76" float was in disgraceful shape yesterday . . . O.K. now, let's go, everybody ready . . . *(As* MURRAY *continues to talk out the window,* NICK *looks up from his work, smiles, picks up a record from the bed, puts it on the record player, turns it on.)* Grenadiers ready, Cavalry ready, Cossacks ready, Rough Riders ready, Minute Men ready . . . *(The record player has warmed up now and we hear "Stars and Stripes Forever."* MURRAY *hears the music, turns from the window, smiling, acknowledges* NICK's *assistance; turns to the window again, his voice gradually growing in volume.)* O.K. now, let's go . . . ready on the cannons, ready on the floats, ready on the banners, ready on the flags . . . *(The music builds up with* MURRAY's *voice,* NICK *humming along with the band and* SANDRA *laughing as* MURRAY *shouts.)* Let's go . . . let's go . . . let's go . . . *(His arms are outstretched.)*

Curtain

AFTER THE PLAY:
QUESTIONS TO HELP UNDERSTANDING
AND APPRECIATION

The first five minutes of the play

A playwright pays special attention to the first five minutes of a play because this section must present a great deal of information to the audience in a very short time. This is the time for "exposing" the facts or pro-
viding the *exposition* of the play, especially the Who? What? Where?
and When?

Referring specifically to evidence from the first few pages of *A Thousand Clowns*, explain what the audience might be able to understand
about the four "W's" of the exposition:

WHO?
The lead characters of the play are introduced, revealing a few major
traits of personality.

WHAT?
The *initial incident* of the play is introduced in the form of a situation
that triggers a series of further situations. In simple terms, one thing leads
to another, but it all has its beginning in the initial incident that starts
the whole plot moving.

Quite often, the play's *theme*, or underlying idea, is hinted at during
the exposition. The hints are often provided by the dialogue.

WHERE?
The play's *setting* often triggers mental thoughts in the audience about
the play's *characters* and the play's *mood* or *atmosphere*.

WHEN?
Sometimes, the time in which the play is set is not important. It could be
any time. More often, the time is appropriate for the dialogue that is
used, for the kinds of situations that are presented, and for the kinds of
characters that are portrayed.

The development of the play or rising action

Following the exposition, the play is taken into its development section
or rising action. It is part of the playwright's craft to keep the audience
interested throughout this development section through the use of several of the following dramatic elements. Try to match these elements,
where appropriate, to examples from the play:
1. Individual characters react to situations, or to the dialogue, often pro-
   ducing the effect of conflict and suspense.

2. We learn more and more about each characters' *goals, motivations,* and *conflicts* through what they say, do, think, and by what others say about them.
3. The audience's interest is heightened through a series of *minor crises* that are produced by conflicts, surprises, and moments of intense suspense.

The climax of the play

The *climax* in a modern play usually comes towards the end. It is usually the play's greatest crisis after a series of minor ones. After the climax, the play may take various directions:
1. It may speed up from its preceding pace and lead rapidly to the denouement.
2. It may change from action to talk.
3. It may change from talk to action.

What do you think was the greatest crisis in *A Thousand Clowns?* What kind of change occurred immediately after the crisis?

The denouement or untying of the knot

The ending of the play is the *denouement* or "untying of the plot knot." Complications are unravelled, one or more problems are solved, one or more characters change in some way, and the audience feels, to some extent, satisfied.

In what ways did you find the denouement of *A Thousand Clowns* typical of the characteristics described above?

SHARING THE RESPONSE

The play is over. The class has presented it in full or in segments. Questions have been asked and answers discussed. Now is the time to "talk it over" as happened with *Butterflies Are Free.*

To avoid repeating the same kinds of discussion questions that were used with *Butterflies Are Free,* the following questions are suggested as "jumping off points" for informal class talk and interchange of opinions:
1. Why did you enjoy or not enjoy *A Thousand Clowns?*
2. If available for viewing, watch the motion picture version of this play and compare it with this printed version. Discuss your preference in these presentations.
3. Stephen Leacock said that "the essence of humour is that it must be kindly," implying that when humour is cruel it loses its ability to amuse. Where do you think *A Thousand Clowns* became unkindly?
4. What do you think was being ridiculed in the scenes involving Chuckles and his kiddie's TV show?

Introduction to
RINSE THE BLOOD OFF MY TOGA

Johnny Wayne and Frank Shuster are Canada's most famous comedians, who have won nearly every radio and television award for comedy. They have written, directed, produced, and taken the leading roles in comedy sketches from their repertoire of over one hundred scripts.

Wayne and Shuster joined forces as school buddies to write and produce musical reviews. They continued with college musicals at the University of Toronto and were the first entertainment unit to enter Normandy after D-Day of World War II. They have had their own Canadian radio and television shows for over thirty years and were the first Canadian comedians to appear on American television with a series of their original sketches for the Ed Sullivan Show.

Rinse the Blood Off My Toga is one of their best-known comedy sketches. It is a parody of the death of Julius Caesar, using the cool, gangster-type style of the novels of Mickey Spillane to poke fun at Shakespeare's tragedy.

The technique of parody is to poke fun at a literary work by imitating it in a different style from the original. Wayne and Shuster knew that their audiences would find the hard-boiled, gangster treatment of the death of Julius Caesar comical because of the way:

—ancient Roman objects and customs are included in this modern treatment of Shakespeare's play,

—Shakespeare's language is turned into modern slang with contemporary references,

—humorous "cracks" are made about politicians, Latin grammar, and literature,

—phrases and situations from television police and crime shows are woven into the plot.

Because this comedy script was written for television production, the following technical terms are included:

AD LIB: dialogue that is made up on the spot by the actors, as, for example, in a crowd scene

AUDIO: the sound element that accompanies the visual portion of the program

115

B.G.:	background sound: the fading of one sound under another
CLOSE-UP:	a head-and-shoulders camera shot
CUT:	the fast switch from one shot to another
DISSOLVE:	the gradual interchange of one shot with another
FADE (AUDIO):	an increase or decrease in the sound volume
FADE (VIDEO):	a smooth transition to or from the black
MUSIC, B.G. UNDERTONE:	appropriate background music played softly under the dialogue or action
MUSIC, DRAMATIC FIGURE:	a longer piece of accompanying music than the "sting" (see below) designed to underline the emotional impact
MUSIC, STING:	the accompaniment of a sudden, short piece of music that has the equivalent effect of an exclamation mark—used as an intensifier for a line of dialogue
PAN:	the moving of the camera to right or left
VIDEO:	the picture on the screen
ZOOM:	an apparent movement towards or away from the object, achieved by using the zoom lens (zoom in; zoom out)

You are now ready for a play-reading or walkthrough production as described with the various plays. The following are the speaking roles in the script:

ANNOUNCER:	introduces the production
FLAVIUS MAXIMUS:	a Roman private eye
BRUTUS:	a friend of Caesar who hired Flavius to find Caesar's murderer

CALPURNIA: Caesar's wife with modern Brooklyn speech

SECRETARY: gum chewing, "gangster's lady friend" type

SERGEANT: a straight military role (has three words)

MARC ANTHONY: a friend of Caesar with a wacky sense of humour

CICERO: bartender for the local gangster's hideout

SCIPIO: one of the gang at Cicero's hideout

GIRL: eye-catching Roman girl

SENATOR: noble, Roman politician (has one short speech)

CROWD: Romans, senators, and assorted characters

Cast the roles for the first, live read-through of the script and include a couple of student comedians who would be able to mouth the sound effects and the musical background accompaniments.

RINSE THE BLOOD OFF MY TOGA

Johnny Wayne and Frank Shuster

Fade in two Roman soldiers facing one another
Title on screen superimposed: Rinse the Blood Off My Toga
ANNOUNCER: *(audio)* Rinse the blood off my toga
Fade out title and fade in on roll: The dramatis personae

FLAVIUS MAXIMUS	TREBONIUS
BRUTUS	LIGARIUS
CALPURNIA	METELLUS CIMBER
CASSIUS	CINNA
CICERO	DECIUS
CASCA	

Fade out cast. Fade in superimposed announcement: This play is presented with
   apologies to William Shakespeare
ANNOUNCER *(audio reading of video announcement):* This play is presented with
   apologies to William Shakespeare.
Fade in next video announcement: And Sir Francis Bacon just in case
ANNOUNCER *(Audio reading of second video announcement):* . . . and Sir Francis
   Bacon just in case.
>   *(Fade video announcement as two soldiers turn to camera and do a
>   take.)*
>   *Cut to: Pillar with sign on it . . . reading . . .* FLAVIUS MAXIMUS
>   Private Roman eye
>   *(Camera moves past pillar and we see* FLAVIUS *at desk.)*
FLAVIUS: Hi. My name is Flavius Maximus. I'm a private Roman eye. *(He rises and
   goes to wall holding a plaque with his number.)* My license number is
   IXIVLLCCDIXMV. It also comes in handy as an eye-chart. If you can't read it
   you need glasses and if you can pronounce it, you're Polish.
   Tonight, I'd like to tell you about the Julius Caesar Caper. *(Indicates bust of
   JULIUS CAESAR.)*
   It all began during the Ides of March. Right after the Festival of Pan . . . the
   god of theatrical criticism. I had just wrapped up the case of Suetonius the Glad-
   iator . . . He'd been fixing fights at the Colosseum. He had a crooked lion that
   kept taking a dive. Anyway, this morning my secretary walks in . . .
>   *(Cut to secretary staggering in carrying three heavy slabs.)*
SECRETARY: Good morning, Flavius . . . here's the mail.
>   *(She drops the slabs on the desk with a marble slam.)*
>   *(Sound: Matching slam of marble.* FLAVIUS *examines it.)*
FLAVIUS: Nothing but bills. Anything else, baby?
SECRETARY: Yeah . . . some guy outside wants to see you. He's awful excited
   about something.
FLAVIUS: O.K. Show him in . . . doll . . .
>   *(She moves smoothly to the door and* FLAVIUS *watches her.)*

FLAVIUS: She was really stacked, built like a brick amphitheatre. Her measurements were XXXVI . . . XXIII and L. I'd hate to think what that would be metrically.

(Cut to the doorway as she reappears.)

SECRETARY: This way, sir.

BRUTUS *(Enters nervously)*: Thank you, miss.

BRUTUS: Are you Flavius Maximus, Private Roman eye?

FLAVIUS: Yeah, what's on your mind?

BRUTUS: Just a minute, are we alone?

FLAVIUS: Yeah, we're alone.

BRUTUS: You sure we're alone?

FLAVIUS: Yeah, I'm sure we're alone.

BRUTUS: Are you positive we're alone?

FLAVIUS: I'm positive we're alone.

BRUTUS: Well, who's that standing beside you?

FLAVIUS: That's you.

BRUTUS: Yeah . . . but can I be trusted?

(Music: Dramatic sting. As we zoom to FLAVIUS.)

FLAVIUS: I could see I was dealing with no ordinary man. This guy was a yo-yo. What's on your mind . . .?

BRUTUS: Flavius Maximus, a terrible thing has happened. It's the greatest crime in the history of Rome.

FLAVIUS: All right, give it to me straight, what's up?

BRUTUS: Julius Caesar has been murdered.

(Music: Dramatic figure. Zoom to FLAVIUS.)

FLAVIUS: Julius Caesar murdered? I couldn't believe my ears . . . Big Julie was dead.

(Music: Sting)

BRUTUS: Yeah, he was killed just twenty minutes ago. It happened in the Senate. He was stabbed.

FLAVIUS: Stabbed?

BRUTUS: Right in the rotunda.

FLAVIUS: That's a painful spot. I had a sliver there once. So somebody snuffed Caesar . . . *(Goes thoughtfully to table and pours drink from amphora.)*

BRUTUS: I tell you all of Rome is in an uproar . . . and I came to you because you're the town's top private investigator. You got to find the killer.

FLAVIUS: I'll try.

BRUTUS: You can do it. You're the guy that nailed Nero.

FLAVIUS: That was just arson. This is murder one.

BRUTUS: Well, what do you say, Flavius? Will you take the case?

FLAVIUS: Wait a minute . . . not so fast . . . I'd like to know who I'm working for. Just who are you?

BRUTUS: I'm a Senator. I was Caesar's best friend. My name is Brutus.

FLAVIUS: Brutus, eh? O.K. Brutus, you got yourself a boy, I'll take the case.

BRUTUS: Great . . . now I don't want to embarrass you by talking about money.

FLAVIUS: Go ahead, embarrass me. My fee is a hundred denarii a day plus expenses.

BRUTUS: A hundred? I'll give you fifty.

FLAVIUS: A hundred.

BRUTUS: Fifty.

FLAVIUS: A hundred.

BRUTUS: All right, seventy-five.

FLAVIUS: O.K., seventy-five.

BRUTUS: Done. Now, my chariot is outside . . . let's go.

FLAVIUS: Wait a minute . . . whoa . . . payable in advance . . .

BRUTUS: O.K. *(Drops coins on table.)* There you are.

FLAVIUS: And here's your receipt . . . *(Hammers away on slab with chisel.)* Received from Brutus 75 denarii. *(Hands it to* BRUTUS.*)*

BRUTUS: You chisel pretty good.

FLAVIUS: Not as good as you. Let's go.

> *(They exit.)*
>
> *(Cut to: Chariot shot driving through the Via Appia.)*

FLAVIUS: We made our way to the scene of the crime through the Via Appia. The street was crowded with the usual characters, slaves, legionnaires, gladiators, courtesans, and sneaky little men who came out of doorways and offered you postcards from Gaul. Before long we found ourselves at the Senate.

> *(Cut to: Senate scene. Senators milling around in a turmoil of anxiety. Enter FLAVIUS and BRUTUS.)*

BRUTUS: Well, this is where the murder took place.

FLAVIUS: You mean Big Julie was wasted right here?

BRUTUS: Right.

FLAVIUS: Well, where's the corpus delicti?

BRUTUS: The what?

FLAVIUS: The corpus delicti. Don't you understand plain Latin? Corpus, corporus—corporum—masculine body.

BRUTUS: Oh, the stiff. Over here.

> *(BRUTUS leads him over to the body with nine knives in it.)*

FLAVIUS: Break it up, you guys. *(Kneels)* Holy Zeus . . . nine daggers.

BRUTUS: Is that murder . . . or is that murder?

FLAVIUS: It ain't Swine Flu!

BRUTUS: Whoever did this should be charged with willful homicide.

FLAVIUS: And practicing acupuncture without a license.

BRUTUS: Well, have you got any ideas?

FLAVIUS: First of all, I gotta make a positive identification.

BRUTUS: What do you mean?

FLAVIUS: Is this really Julius Caesar? Have you got a coin on you?

> *(BRUTUS, puzzled, hands FLAVIUS a coin. FLAVIUS studies coin and body.)*

FLAVIUS: Yeah, that's him.

> *(BRUTUS takes coin . . . looks at it.)*

BRUTUS: Doesn't look like him?

FLAVIUS: That's tails.

BRUTUS: All right, Flavius, get moving.

FLAVIUS: All right, fill me in on the set-up. Who are those shifty-looking characters over there?

> *(Cuts to group, then back.)*

BRUTUS: Shifty-looking? Those are Senators.

FLAVIUS: That explains it.

BRUTUS: They were all here when it happened. *(Cut to individual faces . . . very sinister . . . as BRUTUS calls their names.)* That's Casca . . . Trebonius, Ligarius, Metellus Cimber . . . Decius Brutus, Cinna . . .

FLAVIUS: Cinna the Poet?

BRUTUS: No, the other one.

FLAVIUS: That's good. The poet's nothing. Virgil he ain't . . . "Arma virumque cane
. . . " that's poetry? By the way, who's the guy with the lean and hungry look?
(Cut to CASSIUS.)

BRUTUS: That's Cassius.

FLAVIUS: Such dudes are dangerous. Looks like he died twelve years ago and
came back for his galoshes. Who do you think is the likeliest suspect?

BRUTUS: That fellow next to him.
(Pan over . . . it is BRUTUS.)
(Then pan to FLAVIUS.)

FLAVIUS: Wait a minute! That's you.

BRUTUS: I know, But can I be trusted?
(Music: Sting)
(Camera zooms in to FLAVIUS.)

FLAVIUS: This case was taking on a new interesting flavour . . . bananas. All right,
you guys . . . Somebody in this joint knocked off Big Julie and you're all sus-
pects!

CAST: *ad libs, protest*

FLAVIUS: You can all go . . . but don't leave Rome.
*(They exit grumbling and CALPURNIA passes them, looks sadly at the
body and places a lily on it.)*
(Cut to FLAVIUS and BRUTUS.)

FLAVIUS: Who's the broad?

BRUTUS: That's Caesar's wife. Her name is Calpurnia.

FLAVIUS: Well, she's a suspect. *(Walks to CALPURNIA)* Pardon me . . . Mrs. Caesar.

CALPURNIA: Yes?

FLAVIUS *(Shows badge)*: Flavius Maximus, Private Roman eye. I'd like to ask you
a few questions. What do you know about this?

CALPURNIA: I told him! I told him, Julie, don't go! Julie, don't go, I told him. But no,
he wouldn't listen.

FLAVIUS: Now, look Mrs. Caesar . . .

CALPURNIA: I pleaded with him, Julie don't go. If I told him once I told him a thousand times. Julie! Don't go.

FLAVIUS: Mrs. Caesar . . .

CALPURNIA: But would he listen to his own wife? It's like talking to a wall. I said . . .
Beware, it's the Ides of March already. But he wouldn't listen.

FLAVIUS: All right, take it easy. Sergeant, would you take Mrs. Caesar home?

SERGEANT: Come along, Ma'am.

CALPURNIA: I told him, Julie, don't go. Don't go to the Forum . . . a funny thing will
happen . . . I told him, Julie, don't go.

FLAVIUS: I don't blame him for going.

BRUTUS *(Joins him)*: Well, what do you think?

FLAVIUS: I don't know. This is a real puzzler. Not a clue.
(They sit on the steps.)

BRUTUS: Cheer up, Flavius. You'll come up with the right answer. After all, Rome
wasn't built in a day.

FLAVIUS: What was that?

BRUTUS: Rome wasn't built in a day.

FLAVIUS: Say, that's pretty good. Rome wasn't built in a day. I'd like to use that sometime.

BRUTUS: You really like it?

FLAVIUS: Yeah.

BRUTUS: It's yours.

FLAVIUS: Thanks. Now, let's reconstruct the crime . . . where was Caesar when it happened . . .?

BRUTUS: He was heading for the Senate when all of a sudden . . .

FLAVIUS: Right. And . . . just a minute . . . There's somebody behind that pillar . . . *(Draws dagger)* . . . Freeze!

> *(MARC ANTHONY comes out. He is carrying a sack.)*

FLAVIUS: Come on out, you . . . Up against the pillar . . . spread 'em.

> *(He frisks him . . . He's clean.)*

FLAVIUS: All right, buddy, what are you hanging around for?

MARC: Why shouldn't I? I'm Marc Anthony.

FLAVIUS: Is that right?

BRUTUS: Yeah.

FLAVIUS: All right, so you're Marc Anthony. I still want to know what you're doing here.

MARC: I just delivered the funeral oration over the body of Caesar. I said "Friends . . . Romans, countrymen . . . lend me your ears."

FLAVIUS: Yeah? What have you got in the sack?

MARC: Ears.

FLAVIUS: Get out of here . . .

MARC: Wait a minute . . . don't you want to know who knocked off Caesar?

FLAVIUS: Yeah. You know who did it? What's his name?

MARC: His name is . . . Ah-ee-ah-oh-oo . . . *(He falls dead with dagger in back.)*

FLAVIUS: That's a funny name. Sounds Egyptian.

BRUTUS: No, look. He's dead.

> *(Music: Dramatic figure)*

FLAVIUS: What a confusing case. All I've got for clues are two dead bodies and a sack full of ears . . .

BRUTUS: Now look, Flavius, I'm paying you 75 denarri a day. Let's have some action.

FLAVIUS: All right . . . don't get your toga in a knot. I got a pal. Cicero. He runs a little club in the Via Flaminia. He should have a few answers.

BRUTUS: That's the idea. Get out among the people. Ask questions. Circulate. When in Rome do as the Romans do . . .

FLAVIUS: What was that?

BRUTUS: When in Rome do as the Romans do.

FLAVIUS: Hmm. That's very good.

BRUTUS: You like it?

FLAVIUS: Yeah.

BRUTUS: It's yours.

FLAVIUS: Thanks. Well . . . I'll head down to Cicero's. See you later.

BRUTUS: Ave Atque Vale.

FLAVIUS: Ciaou baby.

> *(Dissolve to CICERO's club. It is a flashing neon type sign that reads: CICERO's Swingles Club.)*

FLAVIUS: Come Singular . . . Go home Plural.

> *(Cut to inside. Camera pans and then cuts to group.)*

FLAVIUS *(During camera action above)*: Cicero's is a hang-out where I can usually get a few answers. It's a small place with a few tables and a trio from Gallia Ciseplina featuring a guy playing the blues on an E-flat dulcimer.

(FLAVIUS comes in and walks to bandstand. Group sings "Hic . . . Haec . . . Hoc" song. FLAVIUS goes to bar. CICERO is polishing a goblet.)

FLAVIUS: Hey, Cicero . . . what's shaking, baby?

CICERO *(Turns)*: Hey, Flavius Maximus; long time no see. What's going down?

FLAVIUS: Nothin' much. What's new with you?

CICERO: Everything's cool. What are you drinking?

FLAVIUS: Gimme a Martinus.

CICERO: You mean a Martini.

FLAVIUS: If I want two, I'll ask for them.

(CICERO pours martini in goblet after shaking it.)

FLAVIUS: Look . . . I guess you heard somebody hit Julius Caesar.

CICERO: Yeah . . .

FLAVIUS: You know anything?

CICERO: Try that guy over there.

(FLAVIUS walks toward man.)

FLAVIUS: Flavius Maximus . . . what do you know about the Caesar hit?

SCIPIO: Nothing much . . . except it wasn't done by an out-of-towner.

FLAVIUS: Local talent?

SCIPIO: Yeah . . .

FLAVIUS: How do you like that? Julius Caesar . . . Conqueror of Gaul, of Britain . . . of all the far-flung provinces . . . the greatest emperor we've ever had killed by a fellow Roman. Terrible.

SCIPIO: That's Ancient Rome, baby . . . you never know when they're gonna . . . do it to you.

(Music: Sting)
(Camera pans to FLAVIUS and zooms in. He shrugs and starts to walk on. Longer shot as:)

FLAVIUS: The whole caper was beginning to make sense. It was a Roman who had put out the contract on Big Julie. Probably one of those Senators . . . but which one? As I stood there trying to make sense out of it all, a strange exotic perfume, a familiar scent I recalled from the scene of the crime . . . *(Goes to woman with back to camera)* . . . All right, sister, start talking . . .

CALPURNIA *(Turns)*: I told him, Julie, don't go . . . I said don't go, Julie, don't go . . .

(He sees her to the door.)

FLAVIUS: You know, I'm beginning to think it was suicide.

(Cut to CICERO.)

CICERO: Look, Flavius . . . I think I know who you're looking for.

FLAVIUS: You mean which Senator killed Caesar?

CICERO: No . . . it wasn't one Senator . . . they all did it.

FLAVIUS: Yeah . . . nine senators . . . nine daggers. But who set it up? Who put out the contract?

CICERO: You mean Mr. Big?

FLAVIUS: Yeah . . . what's his name?

CICERO: His name is . . . Aaaaaahahahahahaa . . .

FLAVIUS: Right, and what's his address . . . Cicero . . . Cicero . . .

(Takes out hourglass and holds CICERO's pulse.)
(Music: B.G. Undertone.)

FLAVIUS: I would never do any more martinus jokes with him. He was deader than Pompeii.

(Music: figure and B.G. continues)

FLAVIUS: This was shaping up bigger than I thought. Suddenly I sensed somebody beside me . . .

(FLAVIUS rises, revealing BRUTUS.)

BRUTUS: Hello, Flavius.

FLAVIUS: Brutus, what are you doing here?

BRUTUS: I was looking for you. Who's that on the table?

FLAVIUS: Cicero . . .

BRUTUS: That's a funny place for him to carry a knife. In his back.

FLAVIUS: He was stabbed through the portico.

BRUTUS: That's even more painful than the rotunda.

FLAVIUS: Et tu, Brute?

BRUTUS: Well, have you come up with an answer? Who killed Julius Caesar?

(Camera moves in on FLAVIUS.)

FLAVIUS: Slowly the pieces fell into place. I put two and two together and it came out I-V.

FLAVIUS: I think I know who did it.

BRUTUS: You do?

FLAVIUS: You see, the clue to the murder was the way it was done . . . the modus operandi.

BRUTUS: The what?

FLAVIUS: Modus operandi . . . don't you understand plain Latin? The method used to kill him. The Gimmick.

BRUTUS: Oh, gimmick I know.

FLAVIUS: Greek he understands. He's probably one of those guys who says etcetera.

BRUTUS: Well, who did it?

FLAVIUS: It's obvious . . . you see there were nine daggers in Caesar . . . and there were nine senators . . . ergo . . .

BRUTUS: Ergo?

FLAVIUS: Don't start up. They were all in on it. But somebody was the ringleader. Now, which one . . . who was around for all the hits? Not only Caesar, but Marc Anthony . . . *(Crosses to body)* . . . and the bartender . . . only one of them, Brutus, or should I say . . . Mr. Big?

BRUTUS: What are you getting at?

FLAVIUS: If the sandal fits, wear it. You put out the contract on Big Julie.

BRUTUS: You're out of your head. I hired you to find the killer.

FLAVIUS: Pretty smart, but not smart enough. All right, do I get a confession or do I have to call in a couple of centurions to lean on you?

BRUTUS: All right, shamus. I did it. I admit. I killed Caesar . . .

FLAVIUS: Buy why?

BRUTUS: Why, because he was crazy . . . crazy, I tell you. He wanted to rule the world. He thought he was another Napoleon.

FLAVIUS: Napoleon! This is 44 B.C. Napoleon hasn't been born.

BRUTUS: I told you he was crazy.

(Camera zooms in on FLAVIUS who looks.)

FLAVIUS: Forget it! Come on, I'll call a chariot and we'll go downtown.

BRUTUS: Not so fast. *(Pulls out dagger and holds it to FLAVIUS' throat.)* I'm getting out of here. And don't try to follow me unless you want to wind up in the bottom of the Tiber in a cement toga.

FLAVIUS: I can't believe it's Brutus talking. Brutus . . . the noblest Roman of them all. Perhaps the wisest man in our whole history.

BRUTUS: I wouldn't say that.

FLAVIUS: Neither would I, but you've got the dagger up my nose.

BRUTUS: Well, don't try to stop me.

(Reaches out and rips a toga off a beautiful girl nearby and drops it on FLAVIUS and exits . . . FLAVIUS fumbles till he gets it off.)

GIRL: He went that way.

FLAVIUS: Who went that way?

GIRL: Brutus.

FLAVIUS: Who's Brutus . . . Brutus, of course.

(He exits.)

(Cut to BRUTUS lashing horse in chariot set, intercutting to same chariot set with FLAVIUS to simulate chase . . . maybe different colour chariots.)

FLAVIUS: Although Brutus had a head start on me, I knew where he was heading . . . The scene of the crime . . . the Senate . . .

(Cut to Senate steps. BRUTUS runs in and darts into temple-like edifice.)

(Sound: Siren)

(Hoofbeats to stop and horse whinny.)

(FLAVIUS runs in followed by two tribunes and a crowd gathers.)

FLAVIUS: All right, you centurions. Let's have a little crowd control . . . Keep those people back . . . and hand me that horn.

(Tribune gives him large ram's horn type bull-horn.)

FLAVIUS *(P.A. amplification)*: All right, Brutus . . . This is Flavius Maximus. It's the man talking. I know you're in there. Come on out!

BRUTUS: Come and get me, Pig.

FLAVIUS: Now listen, you jive turkey . . . you haven't got a chance. I've got the Senate surrounded. Throw down your sword and come out with your hands up.

BRUTUS: Come and get me, Fuzz.

FLAVIUS: Get smart, Brutus . . . we can smoke you out . . .

BRUTUS: I'd like to see you try, Flatfoot.

FLAVIUS: All right, get me the incense.

BRUTUS: Incense?

(Cut to FLAVIUS . . . he throws a smoking brazier or something.)

(Sound: crash of glass)

(Crowd Shots)

(Cut to BRUTUS coughing as he comes out of a smoke-filled temple.)

(Music: Dramatic)

FLAVIUS *(Grabs him and holds a dagger to him)*: Freeze . . . one false move and I'll fill you full of bronze.

(Two tribunes come and grab his arms.)

BRUTUS: You got me, Fuzz. But I'll be back.

FLAVIUS: I don't think so. This isn't a series. All right, read him his rights . . . cuff him . . . and book him.

BRUTUS: I'll be back. Just remember . . . all roads lead to Rome.

(He starts to exit with tribunes but FLAVIUS goes after him and stops him.)

FLAVIUS: Hey, what was that one?

BRUTUS: All roads lead to Rome.

FLAVIUS: Hey, that's the best. All roads lead to Rome.

BRUTUS: You like it . . .

FLAVIUS: Yeah . . .

BRUTUS: Well, you can't have it.

SENATOR: Good work, Flavius. All Rome salutes you. Hail Flavius.

CROWD: Hail Flavius.

FLAVIUS: Thank you. And now, if you'll excuse me, I have a note from an unknown admirer inviting me out to dinner. You sure your husband won't mind . . . ?

CALPURNIA: Frankly, I don't care. I told him, Julie don't go. Don't go Julie, I said . . . but would he listen . . . ?

FLAVIUS *(Puts up his hand)*: You know you have the right to remain silent.

CALPURNIA: Nevertheless . . . I told him Julie don't go . . .

   (Music: Sneak in during above, to finish.)

AFTER THE PLAY: ACTIVITIES

UNDERSTANDING THE HUMOUR

Just in case anyone in the class missed some of the laugh lines or situations in *Rinse the Blood Off My Toga*, try the rapid round-the-class ten-point humour quiz that follows. Take turns in explaining why these lines or situations might produce a laugh:

1. "This play is presented with apologies to William Shakespeare . . . and Sir Francis Bacon just in case."
2. Pillar with a sign reading: Flavius Maximus, Private Roman Eye.
3. "It all began during the Ides of March. Right after the Festival of Pan . . . the god of theatrical criticism."
4. "Big Julie was dead."
5. "You can do it. You're the guy that nailed Nero." "That was just arson. This is murder one."
6. "I told him, Julie, don't go. If I told him once I told him a thousand times. Julie! Don't go."
7. "His name is . . . Ah-ee--ah--oh--." (He falls dead) "That's a funny name. Sounds Egyptian."
8. "All right . . . don't get your toga in a knot."
9. *Dissolve to* CICERO'S *club. It is a flashing neon type sign that reads:* Cicero's Swingles Club.
10. "Gimme a Martinus."
    "You mean a Martini."
    "If I want two I'll ask for them."

CASTING THE PLAY FOR COMEDY

Choose members of the class whom you think could project the characters in the sketch.

Assuming that you were giving advice as a Director to your cast, what would you say to each of the players regarding the voice, manner, and facial expression they might use?

Why do you think the ability to *react* with facial expression would be an essential quality for this type of play?

BRAINSTORMING THE PRODUCTION

Once the cast has been chosen, the rest of the class can assume the role of a production team who oversees the rehearsals and suggests ways of polishing the comic elements while the rehearsals are in the rough, practice stages.

Choose a Director who will use the rest of the class as his or her advisors.

Choose a Script Assistant who will make notes of all the suggestions as the rehearsals proceed. This assistant will have the acting script complete with these marginal production notes added.

Decide whether you are going to present the play live or on videotape. Choose a technical crew who will handle simple pieces of scenery, props, sound effects, and music. The finished product could then be presented to another class to check whether the production ideas "worked."

To involve more students in the actual production, have two groups produce the sketch independently.

BENEFITTING FROM THE TRYOUT

Because you can never tell how well you have produced a comedy until a live audience rewards you with its laughter, try out your play for the first time before another class, using the non-participant members of your own class as evaluators. Then return to discuss their comments and suggestions for improvement. Here are some questions you might use to direct the discussion:

1. Which comic sequences succeeded and which "bombed" and why?
2. Where did the timing need tightening up and where did it need slowing down?
3. Where were the reactions just right and where were they either underdone or overdone?
4. Which sound effects or musical accompaniments succeeded as humour and which did not? Why?
5. Which bits of additional stage business that were not in the original script produced laughter?

Revise the acting script, incorporating the revisions in a final improved production. Present it, after a rehearsal, for the school at a noon rally or take the videotaped version to a nearby school as an English class visit. And, as the actors say, "break a leg."

WRITING AND ACTING YOUR OWN COMEDY SKETCHES

Try creating your own parodies of well-known stories. They need only be five minutes long and in their simplest form can be scripted for Narrator and comic actors who mime to the Narrator's telling of the story.

Questions on
BUTTERFLIES ARE FREE

1. What specific information is suggested to the audience by the apartment setting that is introduced at the opening of the play?
2. Fill in the missing voice of Don's mother on the telephone during the telephone conversation in the opening scene.
3. Don has to pretend to his mother that he had a party to prevent her thinking he is lonely. She is probably confusing the two words "alone" and "lonely." What do you think is the difference between the meaning of these two words?
4. When Jill says, "I just can't be committed or involved" what does Don mean when he replies, "I understand but I don't agree"?
5. What is the irony of situation illustrated by Jill's not being able to find the laundry and Don's offering to show her where it is?
6. The situation of Don's mother entering to find her son with Jill at the end of Act One is called "an effective curtain." What do you think is meant by this phrase, given the situation at which the curtain comes down at the end of this act?
7. The whole of Act Two gradually unfolds the elements of conflict that exist between Don and his mother. Extract any ten of these conflict elements from this act and decide whether the conflicts were solved or not.
8. What does Don's mother mean when she says about Jill, "I don't dislike her. I just wish she were a different sort of girl"?
9. Why does Don tell his mother that he does not like to be called Donny?
10. What are your opinions of Ralph's statement that all things that are a part of life are suitable for including in a play?
11. When Don's mother refuses to take him home after Jill has left with Ralph, what is she trying to do for her son?
12. What does Jill mean when she said that she had to leave instead of saying that she wanted to leave?
13. What happened to make Jill change her mind, at the end of the play, and return to Don?

Questions on
A THOUSAND CLOWNS

1. In the first three pages of dialogue, points of satire are immediately established. Describe what is being satirized in any three points of satire that you identify.

2. Murray spends a great portion of the first part of Act One avoiding Nick's efforts to persuade him to go out and find a job. Describe three different ways in which Murray practises this game of avoidance.

3. Costume and props are always essential symbols of characterization for actors on a stage. What do you think is symbolized by Albert's small briefcase and by Sandra's wearing of clothes suited to a much older woman?

4. One of the major ways in which laughs are introduced throughout the initial interview between the Welfare team and Murray is through the use of ridicule. Describe any five examples of the way Murray ridicules Albert Amundsen's ideas about bringing up young children.

5. Why do you think the audience laughs when Sandra and Albert have their private conferences during Act One?

6. When Murray says to Sandra at the end of Act One, "It's just there's all these Sandras running around who you never met before," what do you think he meant?

7. Why would one judge the end of Act One to be "an effective curtain," which is a playwright's way of bringing an act to a dramatic close?

8. When Albert returns in Act Two to tell Murray that the Welfare Board has decided to remove Nick from Murray's care, he reveals his true character in a long speech. What do we now learn about Albert that we did not know before?

9. On the surface, Murray was just too much of a joker for those in charge of the Chuckles the Chipmunk show. Deeper down, Murray was trying to express some thoughts about the world of children. What were some of these thoughts?

10. What precisely is being satirized when Murray reacts to Sandra's redecorating of his apartment by saying, "I've been attacked by the Ladies' Home Journal"?

11. What is your personal reaction to Sandra's summing up of Murray

as, "Maybe you're wonderfully independent, Murray, or maybe, maybe you're the most extraordinarily selfish person I've ever met"?

12. In Act Three, the poignant dialogue between Murray and Arnold ends with Arnold's summing up of the basic difference between himself and his brother, "I'm lucky. I'm gifted. I have a talent for surrender. I'm at peace, but you are cursed." Explain in some detail the meaning behind this remark.

13. In what way is Leo Herman a tragi-comical character who is more likely to move an audience to tears than to laughter?

14. With which character in this play do you sympathize the most? Why?

Aspects of
COMEDY TECHNIQUE AND
LITERARY TERMS : A GLOSSARY

Bathos

The audience is led to expect an important dramatic event but instead something ridiculous happens.
Example: As the king is being crowned, he has an attack of the hiccoughs.

Comedy

A play that uses humorous characters and incidents and which ends happily.
Example: *Butterflies Are Free.*

Comedy of character

A comedy that produces its humour through the use of amusing character traits.
Example: Television comedies that rely more on laughter-producing characters than on events, that is, we laugh the most at the *way* in which the characters say and do things, rather than at *what* they actually say.

Comedy of manners

A type of comedy that makes fun of social rather than individual habits and customs.
Example: The kind of comedy that could be produced if a group of sophisticated people went to live with a primitive tribe of natives in the Amazon jungle.

Comedy of situation

A comedy that produces its humour primarily through the use of amusing incidents.
Example: Television's series of "situation comedies" that rely on such

situations as students and teachers placed in humorous predicaments.

Comic foil

The use of a character who, by contrast, brings out the comic qualities of another character (or of other characters).
Example: Any "straight man" in a pair of comedians. (Who would be today's Laurel and Hardy or Abbott and Costello?)

Comic relief

The placing of a humorous scene after a more serious scene in order to relieve the dramatic seriousness.
Example: Bottom and his company of Athenian tradesmen in Shakespeare's *A Midsummer Night's Dream* relieve the more serious, romantic complications of the courtly lovers.

Domestic comedy

A type of comedy that is set in the surroundings of everyday family life.
Example: Television's *All in the Family.*

Exaggeration

The deliberate magnification of amusing character traits, speech, or actions in order to produce laughter.
Note: this is a tricky technique since, when overdone, it may lead to an audience's rejection of the humour.
Example: In Paddy Chayefsky's play *Marty*, Marty's mother and Aunt Catherine provide laughter when their Italian emphasis on the need for Marty to get married and have lots of children is magnified.

Fantasy

A type of comedy that relies on very imaginative, fanciful situations.
Example: Lewis Carroll's *Alice in Wonderland* (dramatized) and many of the Walt Disney full-length feature movies.

Farce

A type of comedy that uses far-fetched situations and behaviour usually involving stereotyped characters.

Example: Leonard Wibberley's *Mouse on the Moon* and *The Mouse That Roared*.

Irony (verbal)

The result of saying one thing but meaning another.
Example: "It must be very easy to stop smoking; many people do it at least ten times a year."

Irony (of situation)

The result of one situation being in complete contrast with another.
Example: A famous high-wire artist, who has never had an accident, breaks a leg on a skate board.

Melodrama

The deliberate use of exaggerated villain and hero types combined with "hearts and flowers" sentimentality, all combining to produce laughter.
Example: Traditional melodramas with titles such as *No, No, A Thousand Times No!* that use the well-worn formula of the innocent farmer's daughter who is pursued by the wicked landlord but rescued at the last moment, while tied to the railroad track, by the heroine's long lost lover, Noble Dan.

Mock heroic style

The treating of ordinary characters and events in a grand, tragic style that mocks serious drama.
Example: Playing *The Emperor's New Clothes* as Grand Opera.

Parody

The imitation of a well-known literary work for the purpose of mocking its plot, diction, and characterization.
Example: *Rinse the Blood Off My Toga.*

Sarcasm

Making fun of a person or state of affairs in order to hurt feelings and create bitterness.
Example: Unacceptable racial slurs and personal "put-downs."

Satire

The ridiculing of individuals, ideas, customs, or situations for the purpose of achieving humour and/or reform.

Example: Contemporary television situation comedies, now produced as social satires, following the original success of *All in the Family.*

Stock or stereotyped character

A character that is so well known as a type that it might well have been taken from the stock shelf marked "teacher" or "detective" or "gangster" or "whizz-kid."
Example: Characters often seen in Westerns and in soap operas.

Tragicomedy

Plays that combine both comic and tragic elements, most commonly seen today in plays that are basically comedies but which contain segments of sadness and misfortune.
Example: The short story *Flowers for Algernon* which was filmed as *Charly* and later became a Broadway musical, combined the sadness of a mentally retarded man with the humour of his naive remarks and his innocent adventures.

Wit

Clever, surprising, and amusing turns of thought.
Example: "If life hands you a lemon—make lemonade!"

Match those aspects of comedy technique described above with examples from the plays in *Plays on a Comic Theme*, and from comedies on television, the stage, or the motion picture screen.